Volume I

READINGS IN
RUSSIAN
HISTORY

Alexander V. Riasanovsky
University of Pennsylvannia

William E. Watson
Temple University

D1085567

KENDALL/HUNT PUBLISHING COMPANY
2460 Kerper Boulevard P.O. Box 539 Dubuque, Iowa 52004-0539

Contents

PART TWO ❖ THE TATAR YOKE

PART THREE ❖ RUSSIAN HISTORY IN
THE MUSCOVITE PERIOD

Preface

"*Readings in Russian History* is a three-volume set of primary texts pertaining to Russian history from the earliest period to the present. Volume one includes texts which cover the ninth century to the reign of Tsar' Alexis (1645–76); volume two contains texts from the reign of Alexis to the 1917 Revolution; and volume three will cover the Soviet period, including Gorbachev's Perestroika." The purpose of using textbooks in history courses is to provide the student with an analysis of the larger historical processes and developments which constitute the "macrohistory" of a particular people, region, or epoch. Our purpose here is to provide instructors of Russian history with a collection of sources which discuss both the events of "macrohistory" and the details of "microhistories," which will aid in recreating the historical landscape of Russia.

Because many historians are concerned with providing students with a sufficiently broad perspective of history, many of the previous anthologies of Russian historical texts have omitted accounts of individual existence that have survived from the Russian past. Human lives are frequently not directed by the processes described in history textbooks, and we have specifically chosen some texts because they reveal the "human element" more clearly than other texts that may have been more frequently reproduced in similar anthologies. Examples of this type of text which humanizes historical generalizations can be found in brief excerpts from *beresty,* or birch bark documents, produced by literate laymen in medieval Novgorod, which reveal the day-to-day concerns of average Novgorodian citizens; *The Novgorod Chronicle,* from which we have culled accounts of natural disasters, thus demonstrating the precarious nature of life in one of the largest and most prosperous cities of medieval Europe; and the tragic lament of Boris Godunov's daughter.

The editors assume full responsibility for any errors (or virtues) inherent to the volumes. As in any collaboration, there was a division of labor in this project. Dr. Alexander Riasanovsky has lectured in Russian history for over thirty years at the University of Pennsylvania, and as a guest lecturer at

Stanford, Harvard, Princeton, Swarthmore, Bryn Mawr, and other institutions. On the basis of that experience he chose the documents included in the volumes. Dr. William Watson served as Dr. Riasanovsky's teaching assistant at the University of Pennsylvania and as his preceptor at Princeton University, and wrote the introductions to the texts in the volumes. The introductions are not intended in any way to replace a textbook. Rather, they are explanations for students of the individual passages in each section. As a result of our experience in lecturing and leading discussion sections, we believe that we have indeed found those texts which have been most effective in communicating the experience of Russia to students. The variations in spelling, transliteration, and capitalization which are found in the texts used in this volume result from the differences in style utilized by the various translators whose works we have selected.

READINGS IN
RUSSIAN
HISTORY

A. Kremelena-gorod, Aula Imperatoris.
B. Kitay-gorod Vrbs media.
C. Tzangorod Vrbs Cæsarea.
D. Skorodom, Vrbs exterior.
E. Streletska sloboda. vel Vicus militaris.
1. Curia.
2. Patriarcheion.
3. Templ. D. Michaelis Imperat. sepultura.
4. Podium Ecclesiasticorum in supplicationibus Imperat. destinatum.
5. Tabernæ mercatoriæ.
6. Tribunalia Vrbana.
7. Fusorii ærementorii.
8. Forum equarium.
9. Balneæ publicæ.
10. Forum lignarium.
11. Viridarium Imperat.
12. Equile.

PART ONE

Russian History in the Kievan Period

Chapter One

ORIGINS

Various East Slavic tribes were among the first inhabitants of Russia, having settled in the forest and steppe region between the Dnestr and Dnepr rivers as early as the seventh century. Some tribes lived a nomadic or semi-nomadic existence, trading in slaves and the products of the forest (such as furs, hides, and amber). Others led a sedentary life, cultivating agriculture and animal husbandry in the Don, Dnepr, and Volga river valleys. Small-scale craft industries were also cultivated in villages and small towns located near the rivers. The pagan religion of the ancient East Slavs included some fertility cults associated with the agricultural cycle, and many gods and goddesses in the pantheon represented natural phenomena (Perun, for example, was the god of thunder). Local and long-distance trade brought the Slavic tribes into contact with other peoples, and some scholars have suggested that certain early Slavic deities may have been borrowed from other ancient religious traditions. Sedentary civilization in the region was frequently threatened by the incursions of various nomadic Asiatic tribes who followed the traditional Eurasian migratory and commercial routes west onto the north European plain.

The first cohesive polity emerged in Russia in the mid-ninth century at Kiev, on the Dnepr river. Traditionally, historians have emphasized the role of the Varangians in the formation of this political entity, on the basis of the semi-legendary entry contained in The Primary Chronicle, *also known as* The Tale of Bygone Years. *The first native source for Russian history,* The Primary Chronicle *was produced by monastic authors (including perhaps Nestor) in the Crypt Monastery at Kiev in the early twelfth century. The role which the Varangians actually played in the formation of Kievan Rus', as well as the ultimate origin of the Varangians, are among the most controversial questions in Russian historiography. The "Norman Theory," held officially by the tsars from the eighteenth century to 1917, suggests that the Varangians (and hence the Rus') had their origins in Scandinavia during the Viking Age. According to "Normanist" arguments the Varangians moved south through the Baltic region into the northern Russian forests and the Don and Dnepr river valleys, exploiting the previously unimportant Slavic tribes. In response to this argument, the "Anti-Norman" scholars, officially favored by the Soviet regime for years, argued that Slavic linguistic continuity through the eighth, ninth, and tenth centuries to the close of the Viking*

Age (ca. 1050) is evidence that Slavic groups were the dominant elements in the formation of a proto-Russian political entity. Some contemporary scholars argue that Rus' *was originally a non-ethnic term denoting bands of Slavic, Scandinavian, and Finnic merchants and mercenaries who operated in the Don, Dnepr, and Volga river valleys.*

The first text in Chapter One is the excerpt from The Primary Chronicle *concerning "the coming of the Varangians." For this and for all subsequent passages excerpted from* The Primary Chronicle *we have used the translation of Samuel H. Cross from the redaction of the document attributed to one "Lawrence" in Suzdal in 1377 (this version of the text is therefore called the "Laurentian text"). The Russian text was edited in 1926 by E. F. Karsky of Leningrad, and translated into English by Cross in 1930. Olgerd P. Sherbowitz-Wetzor revised the Cross translation in 1953 for the Medieval Academy of America, of Cambridge, Massachusetts.*

✢ *The Coming of the Varangians*[1]

6367 (859). The Varangians from beyond the sea imposed tribute upon the Chuds, the Slavs, the Merians, the Ves', and the Krivichians. But the Khazars imposed it upon the Polyanians, the Severians, and the Vyatichians, and collected a white squirrel-skin from each hearth.

6368–6370 (860–862). The tributaries of the Varangians drove them back beyond the sea and, refusing them further tribute, set out to govern themselves. There was no law among them, but tribe rose against tribe. Discord thus ensued among them, and they began to war one against another. They said to themselves, "Let us seek a prince who may rule over us and judge us according to the Law." They accordingly went overseas to the Varangian Russes: these particular Varangians were known as Russes, just as some are called Swedes, and others Normans, English, and Gotlanders, for they were thus named. The Chuds, the Slavs, the Krivichians, and the Ves' then said to the people of Rus', "Our land is great and rich, but there is no order in it. Come to rule and reign over us." They thus selected three brothers, with their kinsfolk, who took with them all the Russes and migrated. The oldest, Rurik, located himself in Novgorod; the second, Sineus, at Beloozero; and the third, Truvor, in Izborsk. On account of these Varangians, the district of Novgorod became known as the land of Rus'.

After two years, Sineus and his brother Truvor died, and Rurik assumed the sole authority. He assigned cities to his followers, Polotsk to one, Rostov to another, and to another Beloozero. In these cities there are thus Varangian colonists, but the first settlers were, in Novgorod, Slavs; in Polotsk, Krivichians; at Beloozero, Ves', in Rostov, Merians; and in Murom, Muromians. Rurik had dominion over all these districts.

With Rurik there were two men who did not belong to his kin, but were boyars. They obtained permission to go to Tsar'grad with their families. They thus sailed down the Dnieper, and in the course of their journey they saw a small city on a hill. Upon their inquiry as to whose town it was, they were informed that three brothers, Kiy, Shchek, and Khoriv, had once built the city, but that since their deaths, their descendants were living there as

---

1. The following passage consists of two entries from *The Primary Chronicle, sub annis* 6367 (859 A.D.) and 6368–70 (860–62 A.D.). The text is reprinted by permission of the publishers from Samuel H. Cross and Olgerd P. Sherbowitz-Wetzor (eds. and trans.), *The Russian Primary Chronicle (Laurentian Text)* (Cambridge, Mass., The Medieval Academy of America, 1953), pp. 59–60.

Photo: Icon of the Prophet Elias, from the Novgorod School. First Half of the Fourteenth Century.

tributaries of the Khazars. Askold and Dir remained in the city, and after gathering together many Varangians, they established their dominion over the country of the Polyanians at the same time that Rurik was ruling at Novgorod.

Chapter Two

WAR AND COMMERCE

War and commerce were frequently not differentiated by the early Rus', whose expeditions south towards the Byzantine Empire and the Islamic lands, and among various Slavic tribes in the ninth and tenth centuries, combined elements of both warfare and trade. The Kievan prince Oleg (879–912), who was perhaps a relative of the semilegendary Novgorodian prince Rurik, extended the influence of the Rus' south and north in the Dnepr valley, gaining control of the crucial areas where cataracts made commercial and military passage possible only by portages. Oleg's military expedition to the Byzantine capital of Constantinople in 907 resulted in an important commercial treaty with the Byzantine Greeks in 911. Oleg's younger relative Igor (912–45), who attained the title of Grand Prince, exacted tribute from surrounding Slavic tribes, such as the Dreveliane (who were ultimately crushed by Igor's widow Olga [d. 969] when she inherited the throne).

Turkic and Finno-Ugrian tribes contested the Rus' for control of the steppe region in the ninth and tenth centuries. The Avars and Magyars moved onto Western Europe and were defeated there (by Franks and Saxons, respectively). The Khazars, however, dominated the southeastern steppe and the lower Volga valley from the seventh to the tenth centuries and were ultimately defeated by the Rus' under Sviatoslav in 965. The Polovtsi (Cumans) then emerged as a dominant factor on the steppe in the mid-eleventh century. They were defeated by Vladimir Monomakh in 1111, but continued to be a problem for certain Russian princes until they were ultimately subjugated by the Mongol Khanate of the Golden Horde (when the Russians themselves had been conquered by the Mongols).

Included in this section are two passages from The Primary Chronicle *illustrating the importance of plunder and tribute, as well as trade, to the economy of the early Rus': Oleg's campaign to Constantinople and Olga's revenge on the Dreveliane (translated by Cross). Also included in this section is "The Lay of the Host of Igor," which is regarded as Russia's national epic. The subject is a military campaign to the Polovtsi (Cumans) led by Prince Igor Sviatoslavich of Novgorod-Seversk (1151–1202) whose goal was the acquisition of booty. The text, produced in the twelfth century, was once considered to be a forgery because of the brilliance of the poetry and the fact that no other poems of the same class are extant. Most contemporary scholars, however, consider the text to be genuine, and it served as the basis for Borodin's opera "Prince Igor." The translation is by Alexander Riasanovsky.*

✤ *Oleg's Attack on Constantinople*[1]

6412–6415 (904–907). Leaving Igor' in Kiev, Oleg attacked the Greeks. He took with him a multitude of Varangians, Slavs, Chuds, Krivichians, Merians, Polyanians, Severians, Derevlians, Radimichians, Croats, Dulebians, and Tivercians, who are pagans. All these tribes are known as Great Scythia by the Greeks. With this entire force, Oleg sallied forth by horse and by ship, and the number of his vessels was two thousand. He arrived before Tsar'grad, but the Greeks fortified the strait and closed up the city. Oleg disembarked upon the shore, and ordered his soldiery to beach the ships. They waged war around the city, and accomplished much slaughter of the Greeks. They also destroyed many palaces and burned the churches. Of the prisoners they captured, some they beheaded, some they tortured, some they shot, and still others they cast into the sea. The Russes inflicted many other woes upon the Greeks after the usual manner of soldiers. Oleg commanded his warriors to make wheels which they attached to the ships, and when the wind was favorable, they spread the sails and bore down upon the city from the open country. When the Greeks beheld this, they were afraid, and sending messengers to Oleg, they implored him not to destroy the city and offered to submit to such tribute as he should desire. Thus Oleg halted his troops. The Greeks then brought out to him food and wine, but he would not accept it, for it was mixed with poison. Then the Greeks were terrified, and exclaimed, "This is not Oleg, but St. Demetrius, whom God has sent upon us." So Oleg demanded that they pay tribute for his two thousand ships at the rate of twelve *grivnÿ* per man, with forty men reckoned to a ship.

The Greeks assented to these terms and prayed for peace lest Oleg should conquer the land of Greece. Retiring thus a short distance from the city, Oleg concluded a peace with the Greek Emperors Leo and Alexander, and sent into the city to them Karl, Farulf, Vermund, Hrollaf, and Steinvith, with instructions to receive the tribute. The Greeks promised to satisfy their requirements. Oleg demanded that they should give to the troops on the two thousand ships twelve *grivnÿ* per bench, and pay in addition the sums required for the various Russian cities: first Kiev, then Chernigov, Pereyaslavl', Polotsk, Rostov, Lyubech, and the other towns. In these cities lived great princes subject to Oleg.

---

1. The following passage consists of entries in *The Primary Chronicle, sub annis* 6412–15 (904–07 A.D.) and 6420 (912 A.D.). Reprinted by permission of the publishers from Samuel H. Cross and Olgerd P. Sherbowitz-Wetzor (eds. and trans.), *The Russian Primary Chronicle (Laurentian Text)* (Cambridge, Mass., The Medieval Academy of America, 1953), pp. 64–67.

Photo: Icon of St. George and the Dragon, Novgorod School, Fourteenth Century.

[The Russes proposed the following terms:] "The Russes who come hither shall receive as much grain as they require. Whosoever come as merchants shall receive supplies for six months, including bread, wine, meat, fish, and fruit. Baths shall be prepared for them in any volume they require. When the Russes return homeward, they shall receive from your Emperor food, anchors, cordage, and sails and whatever else is needed for the journey."

The Greeks accepted these stipulations, and the Emperors and all the courtiers declared:

"If Russes come hither without merchandise, they shall receive no provisions. Your prince shall personally lay injunction upon such Russes as journey hither that they shall do no violence in the towns and throughout our territory. Such Russes as arrive here shall dwell in the St. Mamas quarter. Our government will send officers to record their names, and they shall then receive their monthly allowance, first the natives of Kiev, then those from Chernigov, Pereyaslavl', and the other cities. They shall not enter the city save through one gate, unarmed and fifty at a time, escorted by an agent of the Emperor. They may conduct business according to their requirements without payment of taxes."

Thus the Emperors Leo and Alexander made peace with Oleg, and after agreeing upon the tribute and mutually binding themselves by oath, they kissed the cross, and invited Oleg and his men to swear an oath likewise. According to the religion of the Russes, the latter swore by their weapons and by their god Perun, as well as by Volos, the god of cattle, and thus confirmed the treaty.

Oleg gave orders that sails of brocade should be made for the Russes and silken ones for the Slavs, and his demand was satisfied. The Russes hung their shields upon the gates as a sign of victory, and Oleg then departed from Tsar'grad. The Russes unfurled their sails of brocade and the Slavs their sails of silk, but the wind tore them. Then the Slavs said, "Let us keep our canvas ones; silken sails are not made for the Slavs." So Oleg came to Kiev, bearing palls, gold, fruit, and wine, along with every sort of adornment. The people called Oleg "the Sage," for they were but pagans, and therefore ignorant.

6420 (912). Oleg despatched his vassals to make peace and to draw up a treaty between the Greeks and the Russes. His envoys made declaration:

"This is the copy of the treaty concluded under the Emperors Leo and Alexander. We of the Rus' nation: Karl, Ingjald, Farulf, Vermund, Hrollaf, Gunnar, Harold, Karni, Frithleif, Hroarr, Angantyr, Throand, Leithulf, Fast, and Steinvith, are sent by Oleg, Great Prince of Rus', and by all the serene and great princes and the great boyars under his sway, unto you, Leo and Alexander and Constantine, great Autocrats in God, Emperors of the Greeks, for the maintenance and proclamation of the long-standing amity which joins Greeks and Russes, in accordance with the desires of our Great Princes and at their command, and in behalf of all those Russes who are subject to the hand of our Prince.

"Our serenity, above all desirous, through God's help, of maintaining and proclaiming such amicable relations as now exist between Christians and Russians, has often deemed it proper to publish and confirm this amity not merely in words but also in writing and under a firm oath sworn upon our weapons according to our religion and our law. As we previously agreed in the name of God's peace and amity, the articles of this convention are as follows:

"First, that we shall conclude a peace with you Greeks, and love each other with all our heart and will, and as far as lies in our power, prevent any subject of our serene Princes from committing any crime or misdemeanor. Rather shall we exert ourselves as far as possible to maintain as irrevocable and immutable henceforth and forever the amity thus proclaimed by our agreement with you Greeks and ratified by signature and oath. May you Greeks on your part maintain as irrevocable and immutable henceforth and forever this same amity toward our serene Prince of Rus' and toward all the subjects of our serene Prince.

"In the matter of stipulations concerning damage, we subscribe to the following provisions:

"If clear proofs of tort exist, there shall be a true declaration of such proofs. But if this declaration is contested, the dissenting party shall take oath to this effect, and after he shall have taken oath according to his faith, a penalty shall be assessed in proportion to the apparent trespass committed.

"Whatsoever Russ kills a Christian, or whatsoever Christian kills a Russ, shall die, since he has committed murder. If any man flee after committing a murder, in the case that he is well-to-do, the nearest relatives of the victim shall receive a legal portion of the culprit's property, while the wife of the murderer shall receive a like amount, which is legally due her. But if the defendant is poor and has escaped, he shall be under distress until he returns, when he shall be executed.

"If any man strike another with a sword or assault him with any other sort of weapon, he shall, according to Russian law, pay five pounds of silver for such blow or assault. If the defendant is poor, he shall pay as much as he is able, and be deprived even of the very clothes he wears, and he shall also declare upon oath that he has no one to aid him. Thereafter the case against him shall be discontinued.

"If any Russ commit a theft against a Christian, or *vice versa,* and should the transgressor be caught in the act by the victim of the loss, and be killed while resisting arrest, no penalty shall be exacted for his death by either Greeks or Russes. The victim of the loss shall recover the stolen property. If the thief surrenders, he shall be taken and bound by the one upon whom the theft was committed, and the culprit shall return whatever he has dared to appropriate, making at the same time threefold restitution for it.

"If any person, whether Greek or Russ, employs abusive treatment or violence against another and appropriates by force some articles of his property, he shall repay three times its value.

"If a ship is detained by high winds upon a foreign shore, and one of us Russes is near by, the ship with its cargo shall be revictualed and sent on to Christian territory. We will pilot it through every dangerous passage until it arrives at a place of safety. But if any such ship thus detained by storm or by some terrestrial obstacle cannot possibly reach its destination, we Russes will extend aid to the crew of this ship, and conduct them with their merchandise in all security, in case such an event takes place near Greek territory. But if such an accident befalls near the Russian shore, the ship's cargo shall be disposed of, and we Russes will remove whatever can be disposed of for the account of the owners. Then, when we proceed to Greece with merchandise or upon an embassy to your Emperor, we shall render up honorably the price of the sold cargo of the ship. But if anyone on that ship is killed or maltreated by us Russes, or if any object is stolen, then those who have committed such acts shall be subject to the previously provided penalty.

"From this time forth, if a prisoner of either nation is in durance either of the Russes or of the Greeks, and then sold into another country, any Russ or Greek who happens to be in that locality shall purchase the prisoner and return the person thus purchased to his own native country. The purchaser shall be indemnified for the amount thus expended, or else the value of the prisoner's daily labor shall be reckoned toward the purchase money. If any Russ be taken prisoner by the Greeks, he shall likewise be sent back to his native land, and his purchase price shall be repaid, as has been stipulated, according to his value.

✢ *Olga's Revenge*[1]

6453 (945). In this year, Igor's retinue said to him, "The servants of Sveinald are adorned with weapons and fine raiment, but we are naked. Go forth with us, oh Prince, after tribute, that both you and we may profit therby." Igor' heeded their words, and he attacked Dereva in search of tribute. He sought to increase the previous tribute and collected it by violence from the people with the assistance of his followers. After thus gathering the tribute, he returned to his city. On his homeward way, he said to his followers, after some reflection, "Go forward with the tribute. I shall turn back, and

---

1. The following passage consists of entries in *The Primary Chronicle, sub annis* 6453–54 (945–46 A.D.). Reprinted by permission of the publishers from Samuel H. Cross and Olgerd P. Sherbowitz-Wetzor (eds. and trans.), *The Russian Primary Chronicle (Laurentian Text)* (Cambridge, Mass., The Medieval Academy of America, 1953), pp. 78–81.

rejoin you later." He dismissed his retainers on their journey homeward, but being desirous of still greater booty he returned on his tracks with a few of his followers.

The Derevlians heard that he was again approaching, and consulted with Mal, their prince, saying, "If a wolf come among the sheep, he will take away the whole flock one by one, unless he be killed. If we do not thus kill him now, he will destroy us all." They then sent forward to Igor' inquiring why he had returned, since he had collected all the tribute. But Igor' did not heed them, and the Derevlians came forth from the city of Iskorosten' and slew Igor' and his company, for the number of the latter was few. So Igor' was buried, and his tomb is near the city of Iskorosten' in Dereva even to this day.

But Olga was in Kiev with her son, the boy Svyatoslav. His tutor was Asmund, and the troop commander was Sveinald, the father of Mstikha. The Derevlians then said, "See, we have killed the Prince of Rus'. Let us take his wife Olga for our Prince Mal, and then we shall obtain possession of Svyatoslav, and work our will upon him." So they sent their best men, twenty in number, to Olga by boat, and they arrived below Borichev in their boat. At that time, the water flowed below the heights of Kiev, and the inhabitants did not live in the valley, but upon the heights. The city of Kiev was on the present site of the residence of Gordyata and Nicephorus, and the prince's palace was in the city where the residence of Vratislav and Chudin now stands, while the hunting grounds were outside the city. Without the city stood another palace, where the palace of the Cantors is now situated, behind the Church of the Holy Virgin upon the heights. This was a palace with a stone hall.

Olga was informed that the Derevlians had arrived, and summoned them to her presence with a gracious welcome. When the Derevlians had thus announced their arrival, Olga replied with an inquiry as to the reason of their coming. The Derevlians then announced that their tribe had sent them to report that they had slain her husband, because he was like a wolf, crafty and ravening, but that their princes, who had thus preserved the land of Dereva, were good, and that Olga should come and marry their Prince Mal. For the name of the Prince of Dereva was Mal.

Olga made this reply, "Your proposal is pleasing to me; indeed, my husband cannot rise again from the dead. But I desire to honor you tomorrow in the presence of my people. Return now to your boat, and remain there with an aspect of arrogance. I shall send for you on the morrow, and you shall say, 'We will not ride on horses nor go on foot; carry us in our boat.' And you shall be carried in your boat." Thus she dismissed them to their vessel.

Now Olga gave command that a large deep ditch should be dug in the castle with the hall, outside the city. Thus, on the morrow, Olga, as she sat in the hall, sent for the strangers, and her messengers approached them and said, "Olga summons you to great honor." But they replied, "We will not ride on horseback nor in wagons, nor go on foot; carry us in our boats."

The people of Kiev then lamented, "Slavery is our lot. Our Prince is killed, and our Princess intends to marry their prince." So they carried the Derevlians in their boat. The latter sat on the cross-benches in great robes, puffed up with pride. They thus were borne into the court before Olga, and when the men had brought the Derevlians in, they dropped them into the trench along with the boat. Olga bent over and inquired whether they found the honor to their taste. They answered that it was worse than the death of Igor'. She then commanded that they should be buried alive, and they were thus buried.

Olga then sent messages to the Derevlians to the effect that, if they really required her presence, they should send after her their distinguished men, so that she might go to their Prince with due honor, for otherwise her people in Kiev would not let her go. When the Derevlians heard this message, they gathered together the best men who governed the land of Dereva, and sent them to her. When the Derevlians arrived, Olga commanded that a bath should be made ready, and invited them to appear before her after they had bathed. The bathhouse was then heated, and the Derevlians entered in to bathe. Olga's men closed up the bathhouse behind them, and she gave orders to set it on fire from the doors, so that the Derevlians were all burned to death.

Olga then sent to the Derevlians the following message, "I am now coming to you, so prepare great quantities of mead in the city where you killed my husband, that I may weep over his grave and hold a funeral feast for him." When they heard these words, they gathered great quantities of honey and brewed mead. Taking a small escort, Olga made the journey with ease, and upon her arrival at Igor's tomb, she wept for her husband. She bade her followers pile up a great mound and when they had piled it up, she also gave command that a funeral feast should be held. Thereupon the Derevlians sat down to drink, and Olga bade her followers wait upon them.

The Derevlians inquired of Olga where the retinue was which they had sent to meet her. She replied that they were following with her husband's bodyguard. When the Derevlians were drunk, she bade her followers fall upon them, and went about herself egging on her retinue to the massacre of the Derevlians. So they cut down five thousand of them; but Olga returned to Kiev and prepared an army to attack the survivors.

6454 (946). Olga, together with her son Svyatoslav, gathered a large and valiant army, and proceeded to attack the land of the Derevlians. The latter came out to meet her troops, and when both forces were ready for combat, Svyatoslav cast his spear against the Derevlians. But the spear barely cleared the horse's ears, and struck against his leg, for the prince was but a child. Then Sveinald and Asmund said, "The prince has already begun battle; press on, vassals, after the prince." Thus they conquered the Derevlians, with the result that the latter fled, and shut themselves up in their cities.

Olga hastened with her son to the city of Iskorosten', for it was there that her husband had been slain, and they laid siege to the city. The Derevlians barricaded themselves within the city, and fought valiantly from it, for they realized that they had killed the prince, and to what fate they would in consequence surrender.

Olga remained there a year without being able to take the city, and then she thought out this plan. She sent into the town the following message: "Why do you persist in holding out? All your cities have surrendered to me and submitted to tribute, so that the inhabitants now cultivate their fields and their lands in peace. But you had rather die of hunger, without submitting to tribute." The Derevlians replied that they would be glad to submit to tribute, but that she was still bent on avenging her husband. Olga then answered, "Since I have already avenged the misfortune of my husband twice on the occasions when your messengers came to Kiev, and a third time when I held a funeral feast for him, I do not desire further revenge, but am anxious to receive a small tribute. After I have made peace with you, I shall return home again."

The Derevlians then inquired what she desired of them, and expressed their readiness to pay honey and furs. Olga retorted that at the moment they had neither honey nor furs, but that she had one small request to make. "Give me three pigeons," she said, "and three sparrows from each house. I do not desire to impose a heavy tribute, like my husband, but I require only this small gift from you, for you are impoverished by the siege." The Derevlians rejoiced, and collected from each house three pigeons and three sparrows, which they sent to Olga with their greetings. Olga then instructed them, in view of their submission, to return to their city, promising that on the morrow she would depart and return to her own capital. The Derevlians re-entered their city with gladness, and when they reported to the inhabitants, the people of the town rejoiced.

Now Olga gave to each soldier in her army a pigeon or a sparrow, and ordered them to attach by a thread to each pigeon and sparrow a piece of sulphur bound with small pieces of cloth. When night fell, Olga bade her soldiers release the pigeons and the sparrows. So the birds flew to their nests, the pigeons to the cotes, and the sparrows under the eaves. Thus the dove-cotes, the coops, the porches, and the haymows were set on fire. There was not a house that was not consumed, and it was impossible to extinguish the flames, because all the houses caught fire at once. The people fled from the city, and Olga ordered her soldiers to catch them. Thus she took the city and burned it, and captured the elders of the city. Some of the other captives she killed, while she gave others as slaves to her followers. The remnant she left to pay tribute.

She imposed upon them a heavy tribute, two parts of which went to Kiev, and the third to Olga in Výshgorod; for Výshgorod was Olga's city. She then passed through the land of Dereva, accompanied by her son and her retinue, establishing laws and tribute. Her trading posts and hunting-preserves are there still. Then she returned with her son to Kiev, her city, where she remained one year.

✣ *The Lay of the Host of Igor*[1]

The black earth
Was harrowed
By horses hoofs,
Sown with bones,
Watered with blood.
A harvest of disaster
Blossomed
On the land of *Rus'*

Downward
Leads Igor'
His warriors . . .
Misfortune forefelt
By birds in the oakscrub!
Wolves in ravines
Conjure a storm;
Earns squeel, calling
Beasts to a bone-feast;
Foxes yelp at Igor's
Shields of vermillion . . .

---

1. The following selection consists of five passages from "The Lay of the Host of Igor," translated by Alexander Riasanovsky. The first passage is a succinct description of the battle with the nomads of the steppe. The poet fortells the disunity of the princes in a prophetic vision of the Tatar conquest. Passage two reveals that, because it is only a vainglorious campaign, nature goes against Igor. The third passage is the lament of Igor's wife. In passage four God then shows Igor the Path of Righteousness. The fifth passage illustrates how nature now comes to the aid of Igor, pointing the way to the Donets river, his route home where a hero's welcome awaits him. Although written some two centuries after the Christianization of Russia, the full text of "The Lay of the Host of Igor" contains numerous pagan references, suggesting a long period of transition from the old paganism to the new (Christian) religion. In this sense, it belongs to both the pagan and the Christian periods of Russian history.

Oh, land of *Rus'*
Suffer your culmination . . .
"Lord Dnepr, the Knowing
Bring back my husband
So I won't send my tears
Seaward too early" . . .

To Igor'—the Prince!—
God points the way
From the *Polovtsy* land
To the land of the *Rus'*,
To the golden
Throne
Of his father" . . .

Then—
Jackdaws fall silent
And magpies don't chatter
but slither softly
on fearhered bellies . . .
As woodpeckers
Tap-tapping
Mark the way
To the river . . .

Chapter Three

CHRISTIANIZATION

The most important result of increasing Byzantine-Rus' commercial and political contacts in the tenth century was the adoption of Eastern Orthodox Christianity by the Rus' under Grand Prince Vladimir of Kiev in 988/89. In the eleventh century a distinctly Russian ecclesiastical civilization developed out of the foundation laid by the Greek monks who introduced the Cyrillic alphabet, in order to transmit Byzantine religious learning, as well as Byzantine visual art forms (icons, mosaics, frescoes, and domed churches). Byzantine monasticism and asceticism were imported into Russia by Vladimir and his son Yaroslav "the Wise" (1019–54). From these early years to the twentieth century, Orthodox monasteries have been important centers of Russian civilization, as the monks preserved many of the important literary and artistic artifacts of Russian history.

Two entries from The Primary Chronicle *(translated by Cross) relating to the decision of Vladimir to convert to Eastern Orthodoxy are included in this section. While certain obvious hagiographic elements were inserted into these passages, the political realities that underlay Vladimir's decision are also quite apparent. The third passage in this section is an early account of the arrival of Greek iconographers from Constantinople taken from the Kievan Crypt Paterikon. The account shows the practical side of ecclesiastical construction, and considers the uneasy relationship between economics and mysticism in reproducing religious art on the northern frontiers of the Eastern Orthodox world. The story was written by Simon, later bishop of Vladimir and Suzdal (d. 1226). Serge A. Zenkovsky translated the text in 1963 from the 1931 Russian edition produced in Kiev by D. Abramovich.*

Evidence exists that the recently-converted Bulgars had warned the Rus' about the Greek cultural hegemony that might follow their conversion to Orthodoxy (and certain Bulgarian monks took Bulgarian texts north to assist in the conversion process). Some Russian clerics wanted independence from Constantinople from an early time. Thus, there was a need to create an indigenous class of saints in Russia as a means of legitimizing the new church (which, however, remained dependent on Constantinople until 1589). The fourth passage in this section, "The Martyrdom of Boris and Gleb," is hagiographic in nature, and is taken from The Primary Chronicle *(translated by Cross). Extreme asceticism has been a feature of Eastern Orthodoxy from the days of the Desert Fathers (fourth-fifth centuries). By depriving their bodies, Orthodox ascetics believed that they were nourishing their souls. The fifth passage is the record of one brother Isaac who practiced an extreme form of ascetic denial in the Crypt Monastery in Kiev, entered into* The Primary Chronicle *(translated by Cross).*

✤ *Vladimir and the Emissaries of Other Faiths*[1]

6494 (986). Vladimir was visited by Bulgars of Mohammedan faith, who said, "Though you are a wise and prudent prince, you have no religion. Adopt our faith, and revere Mahomet." Vladimir inquired what was the nature of their religion. They replied that they believed in God, and that Mahomet instructed them to practice circumcision, to eat no pork, to drink no wine, and, after death, promised them complete fulfillment of their carnal desires. "Mahomet," they asserted, "will give each man seventy fair women. He may choose one fair one, and upon that woman will Mahomet confer the charms of them all, and she shall be his wife. Mahomet promises that one may then satisfy every desire, but whoever is poor in this world will be no different in the next." They also spoke other false things which out of modesty may not be written down. Vladimir listened to them, for he was fond of women and indulgence, regarding which he heard with pleasure. But circumcision and abstinence from pork and wine were disagreeable to him. "Drinking," said he, "is the joy of the Russes. We cannot exist without that pleasure."

Then came the Germans, asserting that they were come as emissaries of the Pope. They added, "Thus says the Pope: 'Your country is like our country, but your faith is not as ours. For our faith is the light. We worship God, who has made heaven and earth, the stars, the moon, and every creature, while your gods are only wood.' " Vladimir inquired what their teaching was. They replied, "Fasting according to one's strength. But whatever one eats or drinks is all to the glory of God, as our teacher Paul has said." Then Vladimir answered, "Depart hence; our fathers accepted no such principle."

The Jewish Khazars heard of these missions, and came themselves saying, "We have learned that Bulgars and Christians came hither to instruct you in their faiths. The Christians believe in him whom we crucified, but we believe in the one God of Abraham, Isaac, and Jacob." Then Vladimir inquired what their religion was. They replied that its tenets included circumcision, not eating pork or hare, and observing the Sabbath. The Prince

1. The following passage consists of excerpts from *The Primary Chronicle, sub anno* 6494 (986 A.D.). Reprinted by permission of the publishers from Samuel H. Cross and Olgerd P. Sherbowitz-Wetzor (eds. and trans.), *The Russian Primary Chronicle (Laurentian Text)* (Cambridge, Mass., The Medieval Academy of America, 1953), pp. 96–98.

Photo: Icon of Christ Pantocrator, in the Rublev Tradition, Fifteenth Century. This icon shows the influence of the Orthodox mystical movement called Hesychasm, as the halo suggests that the sacredness of the image cannot be captured in material terms.

then asked where their native land was, and they replied that it was in Jerusalem. When Vladimir inquired where that was, they made answer, "God was angry at our forefathers, and scattered us among the gentiles on account of our sins. Our land was then given to the Christians." The Prince then demanded, "How can you hope to teach others while you yourselves are cast out and scattered abroad by the hand of God? If God loved you and your faith, you would not be thus dispersed in foreign lands. Do you expect us to accept that fate also?"

Then the Greeks sent to Vladimir a scholar, who spoke thus: "We have heard that the Bulgarians came and urged you to adopt their faith, which pollutes heaven and earth. They are accursed above all men, like Sodom and Gomorrah, upon which the Lord let fall burning stones, and which he buried and submerged. The day of destruction likewise awaits these men, on which the Lord will come to judge the earth, and to destroy all those who do evil and abomination. For they moisten their excrement, and pour the water into their mouths, and anoint their beards with it, remembering Mahomet. The women also perform this same abomination, and even worse ones." Vladimir, upon hearing their statements, spat upon the earth, saying, "This is a vile thing."

Then the scholar said, "We have likewise heard how men came from Rome to convert you to their faith. It differs but little from ours, for they commune with wafers, called *oplatki,* which God did not give them, for he ordained that we should commune with bread. For when he had taken bread, the Lord gave it to his disciples, saying, 'This is my body broken for you.' Likewise he took the cup, and said, 'This is my blood of the New Testament.' They do not so act, for they have modified the faith." Then Vladimir remarked that the Jews had come into his presence and had stated that the Germans and the Greeks believed in him whom they crucified. To this the scholar replied, "Of a truth we believe in him. For some of the prophets foretold that God should be incarnate, and others that he should be crucified and buried, but arise on the third day and ascend into heaven. "For the Jews killed the prophets, and still others they persecuted. When their prophecy was fulfilled, our Lord came down to earth, was crucified, arose again, and ascended into heaven. He awaited their repentance for forty-six years, but they did not repent, so that the Lord let loose the Romans upon them. Their cities were destroyed, and they were scattered among the gentiles, under whom they are now in servitude."

✣ *Vladimir's Emissaries and the Siege of Kherson[1]*

6495 (987). Vladimir summoned together his boyars and the city-elders, and said to them, "Behold, the Bulgars came before me urging me to accept their religion. Then came the Germans and praised their own faith; and after them came the Jews. Finally the Greeks appeared, criticizing all other faiths but commending their own, and they spoke at length, telling the history of the whole world from its beginning. Their words were artful, and it was wondrous to listen and pleasant to hear them. They preach the existence of another world. 'Whoever adopts our religion and then dies shall arise and live forever. But whosoever embraces another faith, shall be consumed with fire in the next world.' What is your opinion on this subject, and what do you answer?" The boyars and the elders replied, "You know, oh Prince, that no man condemns his own possessions, but praises them instead. If you desire to make certain, you have servants at your disposal. Send them to inquire about the ritual of each and how he worships God."

Their counsel pleased the prince and all the people, so that they chose good and wise men to the number of ten, and directed them to go first among the Bulgars and inspect their faith. The emissaries went their way, and when they arrived at their destination they beheld the disgraceful actions of the Bulgars and their worship in the mosque; then they returned to their country. Vladimir then instructed them to go likewise among the Germans, and examine their faith, and finally to visit the Greeks. They thus went into Germany, and after viewing the German ceremonial, they proceeded to Tsar'grad, where they appeared before the Emperor. He inquired on what mission they had come, and they reported to him all that had occurred. When the Emperor heard their words, he rejoiced, and did them great honor on that very day.

On the morrow, the Emperor sent a message to the Patriarch to inform him that a Russian delegation had arrived to examine the Greek faith, and directed him to prepare the church and the clergy, and to array himself in his sacerdotal robes, so that the Russes might behold the glory of the God of the Greeks. When the Patriarch received these commands, he bade the clergy assemble, and they performed the customary rites. They burned incense, and the choirs sang hymns. The Emperor accompanied the Russes to the church, and placed them in a wide space, calling their attention to the beauty of the

---

1. The following passage consists of entries from *The Primary Chronicle, sub annis* 6495–96 (987–88 A.D.). Reprinted by permission of the publishers from Samuel H. Cross and Olgerd P. Sherbowitz-Wetzor (eds. and trans.), *The Russian Primary Chronicle (Laurentian Text)* (Cambridge, Mass., The Medieval Academy of America, 1953, pp. 110–113.

edifice, the chanting, and the pontifical services and the ministry of the deacons, while he explained to them the worship of his God. The Russes were astonished, and in their wonder praised the Greek ceremonial. Then the Emperors Basil and Constantine invited the envoys to their presence, and said, "Go hence to your native country," and dismissed them with valuable presents and great honor.

Thus they returned to their own country, and the Prince called together his boyars and the elders. Vladimir then announced the return of the envoys who had been sent out, and suggested that their report be heard. He thus commanded them to speak out before his retinue. The envoys reported, "When we journeyed among the Bulgars, we beheld how they worship in their temple, called a mosque, while they stand ungirt. The Bulgar bows, sits down, looks hither and thither like one possessed, and there is no happiness among them, but instead only sorrow and a dreadful stench. Their religion is not good. Then we went among the Germans, and saw them performing many ceremonies in their temples; but we beheld no glory there. Then we went to Greece, and the Greeks led us to the edifices where they worship their God, and we knew not whether we were in heaven or on earth. For on earth there is no such splendor or such beauty, and we are at a loss how to describe it. We only know that God dwells there among men, and their service is fairer than the ceremonies of other nations. For we cannot forget that beauty. Every man, after tasting something sweet, is afterward unwilling to accept that which is bitter, and therefore we cannot dwell longer here." Then the boyars spoke and said, "If the Greek faith were evil, it would not have been adopted by your grandmother Olga who was wiser than all other men." Vladimir then inquired where they should all accept baptism, and they replied that the decision rested with him.

After a year had passed, in 6496 (988), Vladimir proceeded with an armed force against Kherson, a Greek city, and the people of Kherson barricaded themselves therein. Vladimir halted at the farther side of the city beside the harbor, a bowshot from the town, and the inhabitants resisted energetically while Vladimir besieged the town. Eventually, however, they became exhausted, and Vladimir warned them that if they did not surrender, he would remain on the spot for three years. When they failed to heed this threat, Vladimir marshalled his troops and ordered the construction of an earthwork in the direction of the city. While this work was under construction, the inhabitants dug a tunnel under the city-wall, stole the heaped-up earth, and carried it into the city, where they piled it up in the center of the town. But the soldiers kept on building, and Vladimir persisted. Then a man of Kherson, Anastasius by name, shot into the Russ camp an arrow on which he had written, "There are springs behind you to the east, from which water flows in pipes. Dig down and cut them off." When Vladimir received this information, he raised his eyes to heaven and vowed that if this hope was realized, he would be baptized. He gave orders straightway to dig down above the pipes, and the water-supply was thus cut off. The inhabitants were accordingly overcome by thirst, and surrendered.

Vladimir and his retinue entered the city, and he sent messages to the Emperors Basil and Constantine, saying, "Behold, I have captured your glorious city. I have also heard that you have an unwedded sister. Unless you give her to me to wife, I shall deal with your own city as I have with Kherson." When the Emperors heard this message they were troubled, and replied, "It is not meet for Christians to give in marriage to pagans. If you are baptized, you shall have her to wife, inherit the kingdom of God, and be our companion in the faith. Unless you do so, however, we cannot give you our sister in marriage." When Vladimir learned their response, he directed the envoys of the Emperors to report to the latter that he was willing to accept baptism, having already given some study to their religion, and that the Greek faith and ritual, as described by the emissaries sent to examine it, had pleased him well. When the Emperors heard this report, they rejoiced, and persuaded their sister Anna to consent to the match. They then requested Vladimir to submit to baptism before they should send their sister to him, but Vladimir desired that the Princess should herself bring priests to baptize him. The Emperors complied with his request, and sent forth their sister, accompanied by some dignitaries and priests. Anna, however, departed with reluctance. "It is as if I were setting out into captivity," she lamented; "better were it for me to die at home." But her brothers protested, "Through your agency God turns the land of Rus' to repentance, and you will relieve Greece from the danger of grievous war. Do you not see how much harm the Russes have already brought upon the Greeks? If you do not set out, they may bring on us the same misfortunes." It was thus that they overcame her hesitation only with great difficulty. The Princess embarked upon a ship, and after tearfully embracing her kinfolk, she set forth across the sea and arrived at Kherson. The natives came forth to greet her, and conducted her into the city, where they settled her in the palace.

By divine agency, Vladimir was suffering at that moment from a disease of the eyes, and could see nothing, being in great distress. The Princess declared to him that if he desired to be relieved of this disease, he should be baptized with all speed, otherwise it could not be cured. When Vladimir heard her message, he said, "'If this proves true, then of a surety is the God of the Christians great," and gave order that he should be baptized. The Bishop of Kherson, together with the Princess's priests, after announcing the tidings, baptized Vladimir, and as the Bishop laid his hand upon him, he straightway received his sight. Upon experiencing this miraculous cure, Vladimir glorified God, saying, "I have now perceived the one true God." When his followers beheld this miracle, many of them were also baptized.

Vladimir was baptized in the Church of St. Basil, which stands at Kherson upon a square in the center of the city, where the Khersonians trade. The palace of Vladimir stands beside this church to this day, and the palace of the Princess is behind the altar. After his baptism, Vladimir took the Princess in marriage. Those who do not know the truth say he was baptized in Kiev, while others assert this event took place in Vasil'ev, while still others mention other places.

✣ The Coming of the Greek Iconographers from Constantinople[1]

Once, several Greek iconographers from Constantinople came to Abbot Nikon of the Crypt Monastery and began to complain, saying: "Bring before us the men who hired us. We wish to have a trial. They hired us to embellish a small church, and we made the agreement in front of witnesses, but this church is very large. Take back your gold (which we received as payment), and we will return to Constantinople."

Abbot Nikon (not understanding of what they were speaking) asked them: "Who were the people who made this agreement with you?"

And the Greeks described these people and gave their names as being Antonius and Theodosius.

But the abbot answered them, saying: "My children, we cannot bring them before you, for they departed this world ten years ago. But they still continue to pray incessantly for us; they steadily safeguard this church; they care for this monastery; and they protect all those who live in it."

Hearing these words, the Greeks were awestruck. However, they brought before the abbot numerous merchants, Greeks and Abkhasians, who had traveled with them from Constantinople to Kiev. And the iconographers declared: "We made the agreement and accepted gold for payment from those who hired us in the presence of these merchants. But since you, Abbot, do not wish to bring to us those who commissioned us, or are unable to bring them here, then show us their images so that our witnesses can see them.

When the abbot brought them the icons of Sts. Antonius and Theodosius, the Greeks and Abkhasians, upon seeing them, bowed deeply and said: "Verily, they are their image! And we believe that even after death they still live and can protect, save, and succor those who turn to them for aid." And they decided to give the mosaic, which they had brought with them from Constantinople to sell, for the embellishment of the altar.

---

1. From *Medieval Russia's Epics, Chronicles, and Tales* by Serge A. Zenkovsky. Copyright © 1963 by Serge A. Zenkovsky. Reprinted by permission of the publisher, Dutton, an imprint of New American Library, A division of Penguin Books USA, pp. 138–140.

And the iconographers began to confess their sins: "When we arrived in our boats at the city of Kanev on the river Dnieper, we had the vision of a mountain on which was a large church. And we asked other travelers, 'What church is this?' and they answered, 'It is the church of the Crypt Monastery in which you are to paint the icons.'

"And, becoming angry, we decided to go back, and started down the river. But that same night there occurred a severe storm on the river, and when we awoke the next morning we found that we were at the village of Tripole, farther up the river, and that a certain power was pulling us always up river. And only with great difficulty were we able to stop our boat. And we remained there the whole day, contemplating the meaning of this event, since in one night, and without any rowing, we went up the river for a distance that usually requires three days of travel.

"The next night we again had the same vision of the church, and in the church was an icon of the Holy Virgin, and from this icon there came a voice announcing: 'Men! Why do you worry? Why do you not submit yourself to my will and that of my Son? If you do not obey, but try to escape, you, together with your boat, will be taken from this place and placed in the church. And know that you will never leave the monastery, but will there receive the tonsure, and will there end your days. But you will be granted mercy in the life eternal for the sake of the builders of the monastery, abbots Antonius and Theodosius.'

"And the next day, when we awoke, we once more attempted to escape, and made a great effort to row downstream; but the boat moved continually upstream. And soon it landed at the shore under the monastery, and of its own accord.

After the Greeks had finished their narration, they and the monks glorified God, the miraculous holy icon of his most Pure Mother, and the holy fathers Antonius and Theodosius. And actually, having become monks, the iconographers and builders did end their days in the Crypt Monastery. And they were buried near the altar, and their robes still hang there and their books are preserved in the monastery for the commemoration of this miracle.

✦ *The Martyrdom of Boris and Gleb*[1]

Upon his father's death, Svyatopolk settled in Kiev, and after calling together all the inhabitants of Kiev, he began to distribute largess among them. They accepted it, but their hearts were not with him, because their brethren were with Boris. When Boris returned with the army, without meeting the Pechenegs, he received the news that his father was dead. He mourned deeply for him, for he was beloved of his father before all the rest.

When he came to the Al'ta, he halted. His father's retainers then urged him to take his place in Kiev on his father's throne, since he had at his disposal the latter's retainers and troops. But Boris protested, "Be it not for me to raise my hand against my elder brother. Now that my father has passed away, let him take the place of my father in my heart." When the soldiery heard these words, they departed from him, and Boris remained with his servants.

But Svyatopolk was filled with lawlessness. Adopting the device of Cain, he sent messages to Boris that he desired to live at peace with him, and would increase the territory he had received from his father. But he plotted against him now how he might kill him. So Svyatopolk came by night to Výshgorod. After secretly summoning to his presence Put'sha and the boyars of the town, he inquired of them whether they were whole-heartedly devoted to him. Put'sha and the men of Výshgorod replied, "We are ready to lay down our lives for you." He then commanded them to say nothing to any man, but to go and kill his brother Boris. They straightway promised to execute his order. Of such men Solomon has well said, "They make haste to shed blood unjustly. For they promise blood, and gather evil. Their path runneth to evil, for they possess their souls in dishonor" *(Prov. i, 16–19)*.

These emissaries came to the Al'ta, and when they approached, they heard the sainted Boris singing matins. For it was already known to him that they intended to take his life. Then he arose and began to chant, saying, "Oh Lord, how are they increased who come against me! Many are they that rise up against me" *(Ps., iii, 1)*. And also, "Thine arrows have pierced me, for I am ready for wounds and my pain is before me continually" *(Ps., xxxviii, 2, 17)*, and he also uttered this prayer: "Lord, hear my prayer, and enter not into judgment with thy servant, for no living man shall be just before thee. For the enemy hath crushed my soul" *(Ps., csl, 1–3)*. After ending the six psalms, when he saw how men were sent out to kill him, he

---

1. The following passage is an excerpt from *The Primary Chronicle, sub anno* 6525 (1015 A.D.). Reprinted by permission of the publishers from Samuel H. Cross and Olgerd P. Sherbowitz-Wetzor (eds. and trans.), *The Russian Primary Chronicle (Laurentian Text)* (Cambridge, Mass., The Medieval Academy of America, 1953), pp. 126–129.

began to chant the Psalter, saying, "Strong bulls encompassed me, and the assemblage of the evil beset me. Oh Lord my God, I have hoped in thee; save me and deliver me from the pursuers" (*Ps.,* xxii, 12, 16; vii, 1). Then he began to sing the canon. After finishing matins, he prayed, gazing upon the eikon, the image of the Lord, with these words: "Lord Jesus Christ, who in this image hast appeared on earth for our salvation, and won, having voluntarily suffered thy hands to be nailed to the Cross, didst endure thy passion for our sins, so help me now to endure my passion. For I accept it not from those who are my enemies, but from the hand of my own brother. Hold it not against him as a sin, oh Lord!"

After offering this prayer, he lay down upon his couch. Then they fell upon him like wild beasts about the tent, and pierced him with lances. They stabbed Boris and his servant, who cast himself upon his body. For he was beloved of Boris. He was a servant of Hungarian race, George by name, to whom Boris was greatly attached. The Prince had given him a large gold necklace which he wore while serving him. They also killed many other servants of Boris. But since they could not quickly take the necklace from George's neck, they cut off his head, and thus obtained it. For this reason his body was not recognized later among the corpses.

The desperadoes, after attacking Boris, wrapped him in a canvas, loaded him upon a wagon, and dragged him off, though he was still alive. When the impious Svyatopolk saw that he was still breathing, he sent two Varangians to finish him. When they came and saw that he was still alive, one of them drew his sword and plunged it into his heart. Thus died the blessed Boris, receiving from the hand of Christ our God the crown among the righteous. He shall be numbered with the Prophets and the Apostles, as he joins with the choirs of martyrs, rests in the lap of Abraham, beholds joy ineffable, chants with the angels, and rejoices in company with the choirs of saints. After his body had been carried in secret to Výshgorod, it was buried beside the Church of St. Basil.

The impious Svyatopolk then reflected, "Behold, I have killed Boris; now how can I kill Gleb?" Adopting once more Cain's device, he craftily sent messages to Gleb to the effect that he should come quickly, because his father was very ill and desired his presence. Gleb quickly mounted his horse, and set out with a small company, for he was obedient to his father. When he came to the Volga, his horse stumbled in a ditch on the plain, and injured his leg slightly. He arrived at Smolensk, and setting out thence at daybreak, embarked in a boat on the Smyadýn'. At this moment, Yaroslav received from Predslava the tidings of their father's death, and he sent word to Gleb that he should not set out, because his father was dead and his brother had been murdered by Svyatopolk. Upon receiving these tidings, Gleb burst into tears, and mourned for his father, but still more deeply for his brother. He wept and prayed with the lament, "Woe is me, oh Lord! It were better for me to die with my brother than to live on in this world. Oh my brother, had I but seen thy angelic countenance, I should have died with thee. Why am I now left alone? Where are thy words that thou didst say to me, my brother?

No longer do I hear thy sweet counsel. If thou hast received encouragement from God, pray for me that I may endure the same passion. For it were better for me to dwell with thee than in this deceitful world.''

While he was thus praying amid his tears, there suddenly arrived those sent by Svyatopolk for Gleb's destruction. These emissaries seized Gleb's boat, and drew their weapons. The servants of Gleb were terrified, and the impious messenger, Goryaser, gave orders that they should slay Gleb with dispatch. Then Gleb's cook, Torchin by name, seized a knife, and stabbed Gleb. He was offered up as a sacrifice to God like an innocent lamb, a glorious offering amid the perfume of incense, and he received the crown of glory. Entering the heavenly mansions, he beheld his long-desired brother, and rejoiced with him in the joy ineffable which they had attained through their brotherly love.

"How good and fair it is for brethren to live together!" (*Ps.,* cxxxiii, 1). But the impious ones returned again even as David said, "Let the sinners return to hell" (*Ps.,* ix, 17). When they returned to Svyatopolk, they reported that his command had been executed. On hearing these tidings, he was puffed up with pride, since he knew not the words of David, "Why art thou proud of thy evil-doing, oh mighty one? Thy tongue hath considered lawlessness all the day long" (*Ps., lii,* 1).

After Gleb had been slain, his body was thrown upon the shore between two tree-trunks, but afterward they took him and carried him away, to bury him beside his brother Boris beside the Church of St. Basil.

United thus in body and still more in soul, ye dwell with the Lord and King of all, in eternal joy, ineffable light, bestowing salutary gifts upon the land of Rus'. Ye give healing to pilgrims from other lands who draw near with faith, making the lame to walk, giving sight to the blind, to the sick health, to captives freedom, to prisoners liberty, to the sorrowful consolation, and to the oppressed relief. Ye are the protectors of the land of Rus', shining forever like beacons and praying to the Lord in behalf of your countrymen.

✤ *The Story of Brother Isaac and the Demons*[1]

There was also another monk named Isaac. While still in the world, he was very rich, since in the secular life he was by birth a merchant of Toropets. But he resolved to become a monk, and distributed his fortune to the needy

---

1. The following passage is an excerpt from *The Primary Chronicle, sub anno* 6582 (1074 A.D.). Reprinted by permission of the publishers from Samuel H. Cross and Olgerd P. Sherbowitz-Wetzor (eds. and trans.), *The Russian Primary Chronicle (Laurentian Text)* (Cambridge, Mass., 1953), pp. 161–163.

and to the monasteries. He then approached the great Antonius in the crypt, and besought him to receive him into the order. Antonius accepted him, and put upon him the monastic habit, calling him Isaac, for his secular name was Chern'. Isaac adopted an ascetic mode of life. He wrapped himself in a hairshirt, then caused a goat to be brought, flayed it, and put on the skin over his hair-shirt, so that the flesh hide dried upon him. He shut himself up in a lonely gallery of the crypt in a narrow cell only four ells across, and there lamented and prayed to God. His sustenance was one wafer, and that only once a day, and he drank but moderately of water. The great Antonius carried it to him, and passed it in to him by a little window through which he inserted his arm. Thus Isaac received his food. He subsisted thus for seven years without seeing the light of day or even lying down upon his side, for he snatched what sleep he could in a sitting posture.

Once, when evening had fallen, he had knelt till midnight singing psalms, as was is wont, and when he was wearied, he sat down upon his stool. As he sat there, and had as usual extinguished his candle, a light suddenly blazed forth in the crypt as if it shone from the sun, and strong enough to take away man's vision. Two fair youths then approached him. Their faces were radiant like the sun, and they said to him, "Isaac, we are angels; Christ is drawing near to you. Fall down and worship him." He did not understand their devilish artifice nor remember to cross himself, but knelt before the work of the demons as if to Christ himself. The demons then cried out and said, "Now, Isaac, you belong to us." They led him back into his cell and set him down. They then seated themselves around him, and both the cell and the aisle of the crypt was filled with them. One of the devils, who called himself Christ, bade them take flutes and lyres and lutes and play, so that Isaac could dance before them. So they struck up with flutes, lutes, and lyres, and began to make sport of him. After they had tormented him, they left him half alive, and went away when they had beaten him.

The next day at dawn, when it was time to break bread, Antonius came to the window according to his custom and said, "May the Lord bless you, Father Isaac." But there was no answer. Then Antonius said, "He has already passed away," so he sent into the monastery in search of Theodosius and the brethren. After digging out the entrance where it had been walled up, they entered and lifted him up, thinking him dead, and carried him out in front of the crypt. They then perceived that he was still alive, and Theodosius the prior said, "This comes from the devil's artifice." They laid him upon a bier, and Antonius cared for him.

About this same time it happened that Izyaslav returned from Poland, and was angry with Antonius on account of Vseslav, so that Svyatoslav caused Antonius to escape by night to Chernigov. When Antonius arrived there, he was attracted by the Boldinÿ hills, and after digging another crypt, he settled there. At that spot in the Boldinÿ hills, there is a monastery dedicated to the Virgin even to this day. When Theodosius learned that Antonius had fled to Chernigov, he came with his brethren, took Isaac, and bore him to his own cell, where he cared for him. For Isaac was so weakened in body that he could not turn from one side to the other, nor rise up, nor sit down, but he lay always upon one side, and relieved himself as he lay, so that numerous worms were caused under his back by his excrement. Theodosius washed and dressed him with his own hands, and for two years cared for him thus. It is wondrous and strange that he lay thus for two years, tasting neither bread nor water nor any other food nor fruit, nor did he speak with his tongue, but lay deaf and dumb for the whole two years.

Theodosius prayed to God in his behalf, and offered supplications over him by day and by night, until in the third year he spoke and heard, rose upon his feet like a babe, and began to walk. He would not go faithfully to church, but the brethren carried him thither by force; they also taught him to go to the refectory, but seated him apart from the rest of the brethren. They set bread before him, but he would not take it unless they placed it in his hand. Theodosius then said, "Leave the bread before him, but do not put it in his hand, so that he can eat of his own volition." For a week he ate nothing, but gradually he became aware of the bread and tasted it. Thus he began to eat, and by this means Theodosius freed him from the craft of the devil.

Isaac then assumed severe abstinence. When Theodosius was dead and Stephen was prior in his stead, Isaac said, "Demon, you deceived me once when I sat in a lonely spot. I must not confine myself in the crypt, but must vanquish you while I frequent the monastery." He then clad himself in a hair-shirt, and put on over this a sackcloth coat, and began to act strangely. He undertook to help the cooks in the preparation of food for the brotherhood. He went to matins earlier than the others, and stood firm and immovable. When winter came with its heavy frosts, he stood in shoes so worn that his feet froze to the pavement, but he would not move his feet till matins were over. After matins, he went to the kitchen, and made ready the fire, the water, and the wood before the other cooks came from the brotherhood.

Chapter Four

LAW, POLITICS, AND DAILY LIFE IN KIEV AND NOVGOROD

Yaroslav "the Wise" (d. 1054) succeeded his father Vladimir as Grand Prince in 1019 after his druzhina *("warrior retinue") had estab-lished his supremacy over his eleven brothers in a series of fratricidal con-flicts. In order to prevent future internecine strife, the succession in the Kievan dynasty was placed on a legal basis by Yaroslav, with the title of Grand Prince rotating consecutively among the elder males in the family. Yaroslav issued the first Russian legal code,* Russkaya Pravda *("Russian Justice") which combined customary Slavic law and some Byzantine influ-ences. Our first passage in this section is the short version of Yaroslav's* Pravda, *translated by George Veradsky from B. D. Grekov's 1940 edition produced for the Historical Institute of the Academy of Sciences of the U.S.S.R. (utilizing two fifteenth-century versions of the text).*

Civil war plagued Kievan Rus' increasingly after the eleventh century when the Russian political landscape was characterized more and more by small individual landholdings, called udels, or appanages. The second pas-sage in this section is a description of the civil war between Yaroslav the Wise and Mstislav of Tmutarakan (d. 1036), entered sub anno *6532 (1024* A.D.) in The Primary Chronicle *(translated by Cross).*

The ruling family was supported within Kievan Rus' by a warrior aristoc-racy, the boyars, whose members could be chosen to serve on the Grand Prince's advisory council, the duma. *On the level of local government, town assemblies, or* veches, *frequently played a significant role. After the great northern city of Novgorod was placed under Kievan hegemony (beginning with Oleg), it was customary for the Kievan ruling family to send one of their princes to govern. In the eleventh century, however, the Novgorodian boyars and* veche *succeeded in creating the unique office of* posadnik *to ensure that the city's inhabitants would be protected from the excesses of the prince.*

From the eleventh century to the late-fifteenth century this city, which came to be called "Lord Novgorod the Great," was an important craft-manufacturing center with commercial links extending from the Arctic and Baltic to the southeastern steppe. The next three passages in this section illustrate life on various levels of medieval Novgorodian society: the munici-pal structure circa 1471 is explained in The Charter of Novgorod *(translated by George Vernadsky from the 1908 edition of V. F. Vladimirsky-Budanov);*

the flavor of daily life is revealed in excerpts from beresty, *or contemporary birch-bark documents, translated by Valentin L. Yanin, and in excerpts from* The Novgorod Chronicle *(translated by Robert Michell and Nevill Forbes primarily from the "Synodal text" [so-called because it was preserved in the Library of the Holy Synod in Moscow] and the "Commission text," compiled by the Russian Archaeological Commission in St. Petersburg, 1875–88.).*

✠ *Yaroslav's Pravda: Short Version*[1]

ARTICLE 1. If a man kills a man [following relatives of the murdered man may avenge him]: the brother is to avenge his brother; the son, his father; or the father, his son; and the son of the brother [of the murdered man] or the son of his sister, [their respective uncle]. If there is no avenger, [the murderer pays] 40 *grivna* wergeld. Be [the murdered man] a [Kievan] Russian —a palace guard, a merchant, an agent, or a sheriff—be he an *Izgoi,* or a [Novgorodian] Slav, his wergeld is 40 *grivna.*

ARTICLE 2. If [a man injures a man, and the injured man] is smeared with blood or is blue from bruises, he needs no eyewitness [to prove the offense]; if there is no mark [of injury] upon him, let him produce an eyewitness; if he cannot, the matter ends there. If he is not able to avenge, he receives 3 *grivna* for the offense and the physician receives his honorarium.

ARTICLE 3. If anyone hits another with a club, or a rod, or a fist, or a bowl, or a [drinking] horn, or the butt [of a tool or of a vessel], and [the offender] evades being hit [in his turn], he [the offender] has to pay 12 *grivna* and that ends the matter.

ARTICLE 4. If [anyone] strikes [another] with a sword without unsheathing it, or with the hilt of a sword, 12 *grivna* for the offense.

ARTICLE 5. If [anyone] cuts [another's] arm, and the arm is cut off or shrinks, 40 *grivna.*

ARTICLE 6. If [anyone cuts another's leg and] the leg is cut off, or the [injured man] becomes lame, then the latter's sons have to chastise [the offender].

ARTICLE 7. If a finger is cut off, 3 *grivna* for the offense.

ARTICLE 8. And for the mustache, 12 *grivna;* and for the beard, 12 *grivna.*

ARTICLE 9. He who unsheathes his sword, but does not strike, pays one *grivna.*

ARTICLE 10. If a man pulls a man toward himself or pushes him, 3 *grivna* but [the offended man] has to bring two eyewitnesses; [however] in case he is a Varangian, or a Kolbiag, an oath is to be taken.

ARTICLE 11. If a slave runs away from a Varangian or a Kolbiag and [the man who conceals that slave] does not declare him for three days, and [the owner] discovers him on the third day, he [the owner] receives his slave back and 3 *grivna* for the offense.

---

1. Reprinted by permission of the publishers from George Vernadsky (ed. and trans.), *Medieval Russian Laws* (New York, W. W. Norton and Company, Inc., and Columbia University Press, 1969), pp. 26–35.

Photo: Icon of Yaroslav receiving tidings of the Murder of Boris, from the Life of Boris and Gleb. Late Seventeenth Century.

ARTICLE 12. If anyone rides another's horse without asking the owner's permission, he has to pay 3 *grivna*.

ARTICLE 13. If anyone takes another's horse, or weapon, or clothes, and [the owner] identifies [the object] within his township, he receives it back and 3 *grivna* for the offense.

ARTICLE 14. If the owner identifies [his property outside of his town] he must not seize it outright; do not tell [the man who holds the property]: "This is mine," but tell him thus: "Come for confrontation to the place where you got it"; and if he does not come immediately he must produce two bails [to guarantee that he will come] within five days.

ARTICLE 15. If a man [engaged in business] claims his share in the balance from his partner, and the latter balks, he has to go for an investigation by [a jury of] 12 men; if [it is established] that he [the partner] maliciously refused to refund [the first man's share], the man must receive his money and 3 *grivna* for the offense.

ARTICLE 16. If anyone, having recognized his [runaway] slave [in another's possession] wants to take him, [the man who holds that slave] has to lead [the owner] to the party from whom he bought that slave, and that party has to lead [the owner] to the one [from whom he bought the slave], and [so they go eventually] even to the third party. Then tell the third party: "Give me the slave, and sue [the fourth party] for your money with [the help of] an eyewitness."

ARTICLE 17. And if a slave strikes a freeman and hides in [his master's] house, and his master is not willing to give him up, the master has to pay 12 *grivna,* and the offended freeman beats the slave whenever he finds him.

ARTICLE 18. And if anyone breaks [another's] spear, or shield, or [cuts his] clothes and wants to keep them, he must pay for them. And if he wants to return the damaged things he has to pay for the damage.

II. The Pravda Of Iaroslav's Sons

[PREAMBLE]. The Law of the Russian land enacted when [the princes] Iziaslav, Vsevolod, Sviatoslav, [and their councilors] Kosniachko, Pereneg, Mikyfor the Kievan, Chudin, and Mikula met together.

ARTICLE 19. If they kill the bailiff, deliberately, the [actual] murderer has to pay 80 *grivna* [as bloodwite], and the guild is not liable. And for the prince's adjutant, 80 *grivna*.

ARTICLE 20. And if the bailiff is killed in a highway attack and they do not search for the murderers, that guild within the boundaries of which the body has been found has to pay the bloodwite.

ARTICLE 21. And if, while stealing cows, they murder the bailiff near a barn, or near a horse [stable] or a cow [shed], [the one who murders the bailiff] is to be killed like a dog. This also refers to [the case of the murder of] the assistant steward.

ARTICLE 22. And for the prince's steward, 80 *grivna*.

ARTICLE 23. And for the master of the stable 80 *grivna*, as constituted by Iziaslav in the case of his master of the stable whom the Dorogobuzhians killed.

ARTICLE 24. And for [the murder of] the prince's farm manager as well as of the field overseer, 12 *grivna*.

ARTICLE 25. And for contract laborer on princely estates, 5 *grivna*.

ARTICLE 26. And for a peasant, or a herdsman, 5 *grivna*.

ARTICLE 27. And for the slave tutor or nurse, 12 *grivna*.

ARTICLE 28. And for a horse with prince's brand, 3 *grivna*, and for the peasant's horse, 2 *grivna;* for a mare, 60 *rezana;* for an ox, one *grivna;* for a cow, 40 *rezana;* and for a three-year-old [cow], 15 *kuna;* and for a yearling [heifer], a half *grivna;* and for a calf, 5 *rezana;* and for a yearling ewe, one *nogata,* and for a [yearling] ram, one *nogata*.

ARTICLE 29. And if anyone abducts another man's male or female slave, he has to pay 12 *grivna* for the offense.

ARTICLE 30. If there comes a man smeared with blood or blue from bruises he needs no witness [to prove the offense].

ARTICLE 31. And if they steal horses or oxen or [some property in the] barn, and if it was the work of one man only, he has to pay [three] *grivna* and 30 *rezana;* and if there were [as many as] 18 robbers, each pays three *grivna* and 30 *rezana*.

ARTICLE 32. And if they burn or break a prince's beehive, 3 *grivna*.

ARTICLE 33. And if they inflict pain on a peasant without the prince's order, 3 *grivna* for the offense; and for the bailiff, and for the assistant steward, and the sheriff, 12 *grivna*.

ARTICLE 34. And if anyone plows beyond the bound [of his property] or beyond a hedge, 12 *grivna* for the offense.

ARTICLE 35. And if anyone steals a boat, he has to pay 30 *rezana* for the boat and a fine of 60 *rezana*.

ARTICLE 36. And for a dove or a fowl, 9 *kuna;* and for a duck, or a goose, or a crane, or a swan, 30 *rezana;* and a fine of 60 *rezana*.

ARTICLE 37. And if they steal another man's hound or hawk, or falcon, 3 *grivna* for the offense.

ARTICLE 38. And if they kill a thief in their own yard, or at the barn, or at the stable, he is [rightly] killed; but if they hold him until daylight, they have to bring him to the prince's court; and in case [they hold him until daylight and then] kill him, and people have seen him bound [before he was killed], they have to pay for him.

ARTICLE 39. If they steal hay, 9 *kuna;* and for lumber, 9 *kuna*.

ARTICLE 40. If they steal a ewe, or a goat, or a sow, and ten people were [in the gang], each pays a fine of 60 *rezana;* and he who rescued [the ewe], receives 10 *rezana*.

ARTICLE 41. And from each [three] *grivna* [of fines collected] one *kuna* is paid to the sheriff; 15 *kuna* goes [to the church] as tithe; and the prince receives three *grivna*. And from 12 *grivna* the sheriff receives 70 *kuna;* [the church], two *grivna* as tithe; and the prince, 10 *grivna*.

ARTICLE 42. And [when the bloodwite collector and his assistants are on their journey for collecting fines, they receive provisions from the population] according to custom, as follows: the collector receives 7 buckets of malt, and a sheep or a portion [of a beef], or two *nogata* for one week; and on Wednesday, one *rezana* or [the equivalent in] curd; and on Friday, the same; and as much bread as they can eat, and millet; and two hens a day; and [they have the right] to put up 4 horses in the stable, and [the owner of the stable] has to give the horses as much [oats] as they can eat. And the bloodwite collector receives 60 *grivna,* and 10 *rezana,* and 12 *veveritsa* [of which] one *grivna* in advance. And if [the collection drive] occurs during Lent, [then the food is fish] and [he receives] 7 *rezana* for fish. Thus, they receive 15 *kuna* a week in cash, and as much food as they can eat; [but in each locality] they have to complete the collection of the bloodwite within a week. Such is Iaroslav's ordinance.

ARTICLE 43. And this is the table of payments for the builders of bridges: when they complete the bridge, they receive one *nogata* for their work and one *nogata* for lumber [for each span of the bridge]. And if they have to repair several planks of an old bridge—three, or four, or five—they are paid accordingly.

✢ *Civil War: Yaroslav vs. Mstislav*[1]

6532 (1024). While Yaroslav was at Novgorod, Mstislav arrived before Kiev from Tmutorakan', but the inhabitants of Kiev would not admit him. He thus departed thence and established himself upon the throne of Chernigov, while Yaroslav was at Novgorod. In this year, magicians appeared in Suzdal', and killed old people by satanic inspiration and devil worship, saying that they would spoil the harvest. There was great confusion and famine throughout all that country. The whole population went along the Volga to the Bulgars from whom they bought grain and thus sustained themselves.

When Yaroslav heard of the magicians, he went to Suzdal'. He there seized upon the magicians and dispersed them, but punished some, saying,

1. The following passage is excerpted from *The Primary Chronicle sub anno* 6532 (1024 A.D.). Reprinted by permission of the publishers from Samuel H. Cross and Olgerd P. Sherbowitz-Wetzor (eds. and trans.), *The Russian Primary Chronicle (Laurentian Text)* (Cambridge, Mass., The Medieval Academy of America, 1953), pp. 134–35.

"In proportion to its sin, God inflicts upon every land hunger, pest, drought, or some other chastisement, and man has no understanding thereof." Then Yaroslav returned and came again to Novgorod, whence he sent overseas after Varangians. Thus Haakon came over with his Varangian followers. Now this Haakon was blind and he had a robe all woven with gold. He allied himself with Yaroslav, and with his support Yaroslav marched against Mstislav who, hearing the news of their coming, proceeded to meet them at Listven'.

At eventide Mstislav marshalled his troops, placing the Severians in the centre opposite the Varangians, while he himself and his personal retainers took up their position on the flanks. When night fell, there was darkness with lightning, thunder, and rain. Mstislav thus ordered his followers to attack. Mstislav and Yaroslav then attacked each other, and the Severians in the centre met the Varangians, who exhausted themselves in opposing them. Then Mstislav came up with his retainers to attack the Varangians, and the combat was violent. As the lightnings flashed, the weapons gleamed and the thunder roared, and the fight was violent and fearsome. Now when Yaroslav saw that he was overpowered, he fled from the field with Haakon, the Varangian prince, who lost his gold-woven robe in his flight. Yaroslav arrived safely at Novgorod, but Haakon departed beyond the sea. Mstislav, however, when on the morrow at dawn he beheld lying dead his own Severians and the Varangians of Yaroslav whom his men had slain, exclaimed in exultation, "Who does not rejoice at this spectacle? Here lies a Severian, here a Varangian, and my retainers are unharmed." Then Mstislav proposed to Yaroslav that the latter, as the eldest brother, should remain in Kiev, while the Chernigov district should belong to Mstislav. But Yaroslav did not dare to return to Kiev until they were properly reconciled. So Mstislav settled in Chernigov, and Yaroslav in Novgorod, though Kiev was occupied by subjects of Yaroslav. In this year was born to Yaroslav a second son, and he was christened Izyaslav.

❖ *The Charter of the City of Novgorod*[1]

[PREAMBLE]. Having referred the matter to the Lords—the Grand Dukes—Grand Duke Ivan Vasilievich, of all Russia, and his son, Grand Duke Ivan Ivanovich, for their approval, and having received the blessing of the Archbishop-elect of Novgorod the Great and Pskov, Hieromonk Theophilus, we, the mayors of Novgorod, and the chiliarchs of Novgorod, and

---

1. Reprinted by permission of the publishers from George Vernadsky (ed. and trans.) *Medieval Russian Laws* (New York, W. W. Norton and Company, Inc., and Columbia University Press, 1969), pp. 83–92.

the boyars, and the middle-class burghers, and the merchants, and the lower-class burghers, all the five city districts, the whole Sovereign Novgorod the Great, at the city assembly in the Iaroslav Square, have completed and confirmed the following:

ARTICLE 1. The Archbishop-elect of Novgorod the Great and Pskov, Hieromonk Theophilus, in his court—the ecclesiastical court—shall conduct trials in accordance with the rules of the holy fathers—the Nomocanon; and he shall give equal justice to every litigant, be he a boyar, or a middle-class burgher, or a lower-class burgher.

ARTICLE 2. And the mayor in his court shall conduct trials jointly with the Grand Duke's lieutenants, according to the old customs; and without the concurrency of the Grand Duke's lieutenants the mayor may not conclude any lawsuit.

ARTICLE 3. And the Grand Duke's lieutenants and justices have authority to reexamine causes in appeal proceedings, according to the old customs.

ARTICLE 4. And the chiliarch conducts trials in his court. And all of them must conduct trials justly according to their oath.

ARTICLE 5. And each contestant may elect two assessors to sit in the court. And once the assessor is chosen by the contestant, he must continue to deal with him. But the authority of the mayor, and the chiliarch, and the archbishop's lieutenant, and their judges, in the conduct of the trials, must not be interfered with.

ARTICLE 6. And the litigant must not bring along with him his partisans for intimidating the other litigant, or the mayor, or the chiliarch, or the archbishop's lieutenant, or other judges, or the members of the Court of Reexamination. And whoever brings his partisans for intimidating the mayor, or the chiliarch, or the archbishop's lieutenant, or other judges, or the members of the Court of Reexamination, or the other litigant, be it at the trial, or at the reexamination of the case, or on the duel field, stands guilty, and the Grand Dukes and Novgorod the Great fine the culprit for bringing his partisans to the amount, as follows: the boyar, 50 rubles; the middle-class burgher, 20 rubles; the lower-class burgher, 10 rubles; and besides he pays damages to the other litigant.

ARTICLE 7. And if anyone wants to sue for a landed estate—for a farm homestead, or two of them, or more, or less—he may not, prior to the court proceedings, come to the land or send his men there [in an attempt to seize it by force], but must refer the matter to the court. And if he wins the suit, he receives from the judge a copy of the court decision assigning the land to him and entitling him to collect damages from the defendant. And the judge may not claim any taxes [but only the customary court fees].

ARTICLE 8. And out of each ruble of court fees the archbishop, or his lieutenant, and the sealer receive one *grivna;* and out of the fees on writs [issued without a trial because of the failure of one of the defendants to appear before the court], of each ruble the archbishop, or his lieutenant, and the sealer receive 3 *denga.* And the mayor and the chiliarch, and their judges, and the borough judges, receive out of each ruble of court fees 7 *denga,* and out of each ruble of writ fees, 3 *denga.*

ARTICLE 9. And the mayor, and the chiliarch, and the archbishop's lieutenant, and their judges, and the borough judges shall complete the conduct of each trial within a month; and they may not prolong the conduct of any case beyond that term.

ARTICLE 10. And if anyone sues another for the forcible seizure and robbery of his land, the court tries first the case about the forcible seizure and robbery and then about [the ownership of] the land. And whoever is accused in the forcible seizure of land and robbery, the Grand Dukes and Novgorod the Great fine the culprit to the amount as follows: the boyar, 50 rubles; the middle-class burgher, 20 rubles; and the lower-class burgher, 10 rubles. Then the lawsuit about [the ownership of] land is tried. And even if that latter suit is postponed [for any reason] by the Novgorod court, the case about the forcible seizure is tried just the same.

ARTICLE 11. And if a litigant wishes to sue his contestant simultaneously for forcible seizure and robbery, and for assertion of ownership, the contestant must produce his counterevidence; and if [the litigant] wins the case in regard to both the damages for forcible seizure and his rights of ownership, the judge hands him a copy of the court decision with regard to both his rights of ownership and the damages for forcible seizure.

ARTICLE 12. And whoever has won his lawsuit about the ownership of land and the damages for forcible seizure, and has received his copy of the court decision, may proceed to his land, [and if he forcibly ejects his contestant from the land] he is subject to no fine.

ARTICLE 13. And if in any litigation a litigant sues another and that other presents his counterclaims, the matter is brought to the court, and until it is settled neither of the litigants may start any further lawsuits against the other; nor may he instigate Novgorod citizens against his contestant. And he shall swear that he will resort to no subterfuge about it.

ARTICLE 14. Anyone commencing a lawsuit [after the promulgation of this charter] must kiss the cross once, [promising to obey the law]; and if he comes to the court hall without having kissed the cross, he must kiss it and only then is allowed to sue; and if the defendant has not yet kissed the cross after the promulgation of this charter, he likewise must kiss the cross and only then may sue; and if either litigant refuses to kiss the cross he loses his case.

ARTICLE 15. And if a litigant refuses to kiss the cross under the pretext that he is represented by an attorney, he has to kiss the cross once just the same, and only then his attorney may conduct the suit; and if he keeps refusing to kiss the cross, he loses his case.

ARTICLE 16. And if the widow, either of an upper-class man, or of a middle-class burgher, is a defendant in a suit, and she has a son, that son may kiss the cross on behalf of both himself and his mother, once; and if the son refuses to kiss the cross on behalf of his mother, the mother has to kiss the cross in her home in the presence of the plaintiff and of the Novgorod constables.

ARTICLE 17. And in litigations about land the boyar, the middle-class burgher, or the merchant, shall kiss the cross in behalf of himself and his wife.

ARTICLE 18. And if they sue a boyar, or a middle-class burgher, or a merchant for his land or for his wife's land, he may, after having kissed the cross, defend himself, or he may send his attorney in behalf of himself and his wife.

ARTICLE 19. And in litigations about boats the attorney and the witness must kiss the cross.

ARTICLE 20. And the same members of the Court of Reëxamination who accept a case shall conduct it to the conclusion.

ARTICLE 21. And when the assessors state the case, the judge orders his secretary to write down his statement, and the assessors seal the copy.

ARTICLE 22. And it is not permissible to produce a witness against [an already recognized] witness. And neither [an alien, such as] a Pskov citizen, nor a full slave may serve as witness [in regular cases]. But a slave may be a witness against another slave.

ARTICLE 23. And if the litigants refer to a witness, the allowance for travel expenses of the officials [sent for the witness] must be paid in advance: to the sergeant, up to 100 versts, according to old custom; to the constable, or the archbishop's squire, or the herald, or the informer, four *grivna* up to 100 versts. And if a litigant refers to a witness whose residence is more than 100 versts distant, and the other litigant agrees to refer to the same witness, the latter is summoned. But if the other litigant refuses to pay his share for summoning a witness from a distance over 100 versts, he may produce his own witness. And the term for summoning a witness from a distance not over 100 versts is three weeks. And it is the loser of the suit who finally covers the expenses for the summoning of a witness, but the amount is paid in advance to the sergeant.

ARTICLE 24. And if there is a litigation about land, and the defendant asks for a term for obtaining documents or summoning the co-owners of the land [from a distance], the term is three weeks for 100 versts, and proportionally if the distance is more or less than that figure. And he must name his co-owners and indicate specifically where the documents are, supporting his statement by an oath. And he has to strike an agreement with the plaintiff concerning the term, and the mayor has to seal that agreement, and the term may not be changed after that; and the fee for a term agreement is one *grivna*. And [if the case is tried not by the mayor] but by some other judge, he has to confirm the term agreement accordingly. And if a litigant refuses to accept his sealed copy of the term agreement, the judge handling the case shall accuse him without waiting for the expiration of the term. And for other lawsuits the term is appointed according to old customs.

ARTICLE 25. And at the court presided over by the Grand Duke's justice there shall be an assessor for each litigant, and the assessors must be reliable men and must conduct trial honestly, after being sworn to obey the law according to this charter.

ARTICLE 26. And if the cause has been referred to the superior court [on the judge's recommendation], the Court of Reexamination meets in the archbishop's hall, with one boyar and one middle-class burgher from each city district present; also present are those judges and assessors who had tried the case in the lower court, as well as the assessors representing the litigants; and no one else is admitted. And the members of the Court of Reexamination meet thrice a week, on Mondays, Wednesdays, and Fridays. And if a member fails to attend a session, he is fined two rubles, if he is a boyar; and if he is a middle-class burgher, one ruble. And the members of the Court of Reëxamination shall accept no bribes, nor favor any side through some subterfuge, in accordance with their oath. And he who attends the session of the Court of Reexamination for the first time, must kiss the cross once, [promising to obey the law] according to this charter.

ARTICLE 27. And the mayor, and the chiliarch, and the archbishop's lieutenant, and their judges, and the borough judges all have to kiss the cross [promising] that they will conduct the trials justly.

ARTICLE 28. And the trial of any lawsuit about land has to be completed within two months; and its conclusion may not be delayed over two months. [But if the boundaries have to be examined by a land-surveyor], the mayor has two more months, following the land-surveyor's report, to complete the case, but he may not prolong it over two months. And if the mayor, after having sent the land-surveyor to examine the boundaries, leaves the city [for some private business] without having completed the case, the Grand Dukes and Novgorod the Great fine him 50 rubles, and besides he has to pay the damages to the plaintiff. Likewise, if the chiliarch, or the archbishop's lieutenant, leaves the city before the completion of the case he tries, the Grand Dukes and Novgorod the Great fine him 50 rubles, and besides he has to pay the damages to the plaintiff.

ARTICLE 29. And if a judge has not completed a lawsuit about land within two months, the plaintiff shall receive, for his assistance, sergeants at arms from Novgorod the Great, and the judge shall complete the case in the presence of those sergeants at arms. [And if the judge refers the matter to the court of Reexamination] and that Court does not complete the case within two months, the judge [of the lower court] and the plaintiff likewise apply to Novgorod the Great for help and receive sergeants at arms [for compelling] the members of the Court of Reexamination [to conduct the case without delay]. The court of Reexamination shall then instruct the judge [of the lower court] concerning the solution of the case, in the presence of the sergeants at arms, and the judge completes the case in the presence of the said sergeants.

ARTICLE 30. And if any litigants agree upon the time [of the hearing of their case] and each of them receives from the judge a copy of the term agreement, and then the judge is removed, the litigants have to appear before his successor and produce their copies of the term agreement, in time, and that judge shall conduct and complete that case.

ARTICLE 31. And if one of the litigants appears before the judge in time and produces his copy of the term agreement, and the other does not appear [he stands accused, and] the judge issues a writ against him, [a copy of which is handed to that litigant who did appear before the judge]. And to that copy of the writ his copy of the term agreement is attached by seal; and no notice is sent to the defendant.

ARTICLE 32. And if an attorney arranges for a term [of the hearing of the case] in behalf of the claimant and dies before the appointed time, the claimant has either to appear in person before the judge in time, or to send another attorney; and if he fails to appear in person, or to send another attorney, he stands accused.

ARTICLE 33. And if anyone wins a lawsuit about theft on the evidence of the stolen object being found in the home of the defendant, or about robbery, or burglary, or murder, or about a runaway slave, or about a land deed, the judges collect four *grivna* for each court decision, and two *grivna* for each writ.

ARTICLE 34. And if anyone [wins a lawsuit and] receives a copy of the court decision, the defendant must pay his score both to the judge [as court fees] and to the plaintiff, within a month. And if he does not settle his score within a month, the plaintiff may apply to the city assembly for constables in order to apprehend the defendant, be it in the city or in a village. And if the defendant hides from the constables, the whole authority of Novgorod the Great is against him.

ARTICLE 35. And if anyone is charged by a witness with some crime, he may challenge the witness within two weeks; and if the witness evades the challenge for two weeks, the defendant approaches the plaintiff; and if the witness hides from the plaintiff, the charges of such a witness are no charges, and the defendant stands acquitted. And if the defendant does not challenge either the witness or the plaintiff within two weeks, [he stands accused], and the judge issues a writ against him on the evidence of the charges.

ARTICLE 36. And if [a Novgorod citizen] charges a man subject to the authority of the archbishop, or of a boyar, or of a middle-class burgher, or of a merchant, or of a monastery, or of a city district guild, or of a street guild, with a crime committed in a country district—such as theft, or robbery, or burglary, or arson, or murder, or with being his runaway slave—the claimant, provided he has been duly sworn to obey the law according to this charter, may present to the authorities his statement, signed by him and confirmed by oath, to the effect that the man he charges is indeed a thief, or a robber, or a burglar, or an incendiary, or a murderer, or [his runaway] slave. And the archbishop's officials in the country district [referred to by the claimant]—the bailiff, or the village steward—must bring that [suspected] man to the court; and the boyar, or the middle-class burgher, or the merchant, or the monastery bailiff or the village steward, or the city district elder, or the street elder, likewise must bring that [suspected] man to the court. And the term [for producing him] is three weeks for a distance of 100 versts, and more or less proportionally. And nobody shall abuse him prior to the hearing of the case in the court; and whoever abuses him, himself stands accused.

ARTICLE 37. And if a man charged [with a crime or claimed by the plaintiff as his runaway slave] registers as the slave of another, the [new] owner may not keep him in his house; and if he keeps him and is detected, he has to pay damages. Nor may the owner send that man away into another country district; if sent away, the man has to be surrendered to the plaintiff. And no country district authorities shall accept that man, in accordance with their oath. [All the above regulations are issued for the cases of this nature only] and in other kinds of cases the litigants deal with each other [without the assistance of the said authorities]. And if anyone kisses the cross and signs the promise that he will not keep that [suspected] man in his country district, [and keeps him] and is detected, he has to pay the damages to the plaintiff. And if the man moves into another country district, its authorities must bring him to the court, according to their oath; and if they fail to bring him to the court, they are fined in accordance with the Novgorod Charter.

ARTICLE 38. And if anyone charges a man subject to the authority of the archbishop or of a boyar, or of a middle-class burgher, or of a merchant, or of a monastery, or of a city district guild, or of a street guild, with some crime, and has not kissed the cross to obey the law according to this charter, he has to deal directly with the defendant.

ARTICLE 39. And whoever has agreed upon the time of his appearing before the court, no notices are sent to him; but if the judge postpones the term, he shall send notices to the litigants. And if a litigant hides from being served the notice, the notice is sent to him thrice, and he is called by a herald; if he does not then appear before the court, a writ is issued against him for the breach of a pledge and he is fined to an amount not over 3 *denga*.

ARTICLE 40. And if [the defendant's partisans] seize the plaintiff in a village and abuse him, his nearest relative or friend receives from the judge a writ in his behalf against the defendant.

ARTICLE 41. And when a claimant summons the other claimant from a village through a messenger or a squire, the term is two weeks for 100 versts, and more or less proportionally.

ARTICLE 42. Two men shall represent [in the court] a city district, or a street, or a hundred, or a row [in the litigations involving inhabitants of any of the town communities]; and no other men are to be let in to the court hall or allowed to take part in the hearing. And if [besides those two appointed men] the defendant's partisans from a city district, or street, or hundred, or row, throng in the court hall, the Grand Dukes and Novgorod the Great, in accordance with this charter, [fine] those two men. . . .

✛ *Beresty*[1]

"Greetings from the priest to Grechin. Paint me two six-winged seraphims on two icons for the top of the iconostasis. I kiss you. God will reward you or we'll make a deal."

"From Nikita to Ulyanitsa. Marry me. I want you and you me. And as witness will be Ignato."

"From Boris to Nastasya. As soon as you receive this letter send me a man on horseback, since I have a lot to do here. Oh yes, send a shirt. I forgot one."

✛ *The Chronicle of Novgorod*[1]

A.D. 1123 A.M. 6631. Vsevolod, son of Mstislav, married in Novgorod. The same year the Church of St. Mikhail fell in Pereyaslavl, and in the spring, Vsevolod and the men of Novgorod during the Great Fast went against the

---

1. Reproduced from Valentin L. Yanin, "The Archaeology of Novgorod," *Scientific American* (February, 1990), p. 87. *Beresty* are letters that were produced on birchbark in central and northern Russian cities from the mid-eleventh century to the early fifteenth century. Judging by the quantity of *beresty* found in Novgorod, the literacy rate in that city was probably quite high.

1. Reprinted by permission of the publishers from Robert Mitchell and Nevill Forbes (eds. and trans.) *The Novgorod Chronicle, 1016–1471* (Gulf Breeze, Florida, Academic International Press, 1970), pp. 10–11, 18–19, 20–21.

Yem people and defeated them; but the march was terrible; [a loaf of] bread cost one *nogata.*

A.D. 1121. A.M. 6632 On the 11th day of August before evening service the sun began to decrease and it totally perished; oh, there was great terror and darkness! there were stars and the moon; then it began to re-appear and came out quickly in full; then all the city rejoiced.

A.D. 1125. A.M. 6633. Volodimir the Great, son of Vsevolod, died in Kiev; and they put his son Mstislav on the throne of his father. The same year there was a great storm with thunder and hail; it rent houses and it rent tiles off shrines; it drowned droves of cattle in the Volkhov, and others they hardly saved alive. The same year they painted the Anton chapel in the monastery (sc. frescoes).

The same year the people of Novgorod put Vsevolod on the throne.

A.D. 1126. A.M. 6634. Vsevolod went to Kiev to his father and he came back to the throne in Novgorod on February 28. The same year they gave the office of *Posadnik* to Miroslav Gyuryatinits.

A.D. 1127. A.M. 6635. Vsevolod founded the stone church of St. Ioan in Novgorod, in the name of his son, in Petryata's Court. The same year a blizzard fell thick over land and water and houses during two nights and four days. The same year the *Igumen* Anton built a refectory of stone in Novgorod. The same year the water was high in the Volkhov and snow lay until James's day. And in the autumn the frost killed all the corn and the winter crop; and there was famine throughout the winter; an *osminka* of rye cost half a *grivna.*

A.D. 1128. A.M. 6636. Kyuryak, *Igumen* of St. Georgi died. The same year Ioan, son of Vsevolod, grandson of Mstislav, died on April 16. The same year Zavid Dmitrovits was made *Posadnik* in Novgorod. This year it was cruel; one *osminka* or rye cost a *grivna;* the people ate lime tree leaves, birch bark, pounded wood pulp mixed with husks and straw; some ate buttercups, moss, horse flesh; and thus many dropping down from hunger, their corpses were in the streets, in the market place, and on the roads, and everywhere. They hired hirelings to carry the dead out of the town; the serfs could not go out; woe and misery on all! Fathers and mothers would put their children into boats in gift to merchants, or else put them to death; and others dispersed over foreign lands. Thus did our country perish on account of our sins. This year, the water was high in the Volkhov, and carried away many houses; and *Knyaz* Boris Vseslavits of Polotsk died; and Zavid Dmitrovits, *Posadnik* of Novgorod, died.

A.D. 1129. A.M. 6637. Daniel came from Kiev to be *Posadnik* in Novgorod.

A.D. 1143. A.M. 6651. All the autumn was rainy, from Our Lady's Birthday to *Korochun* warm wet; and the water was very high in the Volkhov and everywhere, it carried abroad hay and wood; the lake froze in the night, and the wind broke up [the ice] and carried it into the Volkhov, and it broke the bridge, it carried away four piles, never heard of more.

The same year Svyatopolk married in Novgorod, he brought a wife from Moravia, between Christmas and Epiphany.

The same year the Korel people went against the Yem people and [those] running away, they destroyed two of their vessels.

A.D. 1144. A.M. 6652. They made a whole bridge across the Volkhov by the side of the old one, entirely new.

The same year the whole of *Kholm* was burned, and the church of St. Ilya. The same year they painted fittingly all the porches in the Church of St. Sophia in Novgorod, under *Vladyka* Nifont. Then, too, they gave the *Posadnik*-ship to Nezhata Tverdyatits. The same year they finished the stone church of the Holy Mother of God in the market place in Novgorod. The same year the holy *Vladyka* Nifont appointed me priest.

A.D. 1145. A.M. 6653. There were two whole weeks of great heat, like burning sparks, before harvest; then came rain, so that we saw not a clear day till winter; and a great quantity of corn and hay they were unable to harvest; and that autumn the water was higher than three years before; and in the winter there was not much snow, and no clear day, not till March. The same year, two priests were drowned and the Bishop did not let sing over them. The same year they founded a stone church, Boris and Gleb, at Smyadino by Smolensk. The same year the whole Russian Land went against Galich, they devastated much of their province, but took not one town, and returned, and they went also from Novgorod with *Voyevoda* Nerevin to help the people of Kiev, and returned with love.

A.D. 1146. A.M. 6654. Vsevolod died in Russia in the month of July, and his brother, Igor, took his seat on the throne and sat two weeks, and the people disliked him; and they sent word to Izyaslav Mstislavich in Pereyaslavl, and he came with soldiers, and they fought; and God helped Izyaslav, and Izyaslav took his seat on the throne; and they took Igor five days after the fight and made him captive; and in the autumn he begged permission to be shorn; and he was shorn.

Then, too, they gave the *Posadnik*-ship to Kostyantin Mikultsits, having taken it away from Nezhata.

The same year they made four churches: to the holy Martyrs Boris and Gleb in the town, to the holy Prophet Ilya, to the holy Apostles Peter and Paul, in the *Kholm* [quarter], and to the Holy Benefactors Kosma and Damyan.

A.D. 1147. A.M. 6655. In the autumn of Svyatopolk with the whole Novgorod province went against Gyurgi wishing to go against Suzhdal, and turned back at Novi-torg for the bad roads.

The same year in the winter *Posadnik* Kostyantin died and they gave it again to Sudila Ivankovits.

Then, too, *Igumen* Onton died. The same year they gave the *Igumen*-ship to Andrei in Onton's place.

The same year the people of Kiev killed *Knyas* Igor Olgovits.

A.D. 1148. A.M. 6656. There was rain with hail on June 27, a Sunday; and thunder set fire to the Church of the Holy Mother of God in the monastery of Zverinets. The same year *Vladyka* Nifont went to Suzhdal, for peace, to Gyurgi; and Gyurgi received him with love, and consecrated the Church of the Holy Mother of God, with great consecration, and released all the men of Novi-torg and all the merchants, untouched, and sent them with honour to Novgorod; but peace he gave not.

The same autumn Izyaslav sent his son, Yaroslav, from Kiev, and the men of Novgorod received him, and he took Svyatopolk away because of his wickedness, and they gave him Volodimir.

The same winter Izyaslav, son of Mstislav, came to Novgorod from Kiev, and went to Rostov against Gyurgi with the men of Novgorod; and they made much war on Gyurgi's people, and took six small towns on the Volga, they laid waste as far as Yaroslavl, and took 7,000 heads (captives), and turned back for the bad roads.

A.D. 1151. A.M. 6659. Izyaslav with Vyacheslav defeated Gyurgi at Pereyaslavl on July 17.

The same winter the *Knyaginya* of Izyaslav died.

The same year *Vladyka* Nifont covered St. Sophia all smoothly over with lead and plastered it with lime all about. Then, too, they erected two churches: of St. Vasili and of St. Kostyantin and his mother, Helen.

A.D. 1152. A.M. 6660. On April 23, the Church of St. Michael in the middle of the market place took fire, and there was much damage; the whole market place was burnt, and the houses up to the stream, and hitherwards to Slavno, and eight churches were burnt down, and a ninth, the Varangian one.

A.D. 1153. A.M. 6661. The God-loving *Vladyka* Nifont went to Ladoga and founded the stone Church of St. Kliment.

The same year *Igumen* Arkadi built the wooden Church of the Assumption of the Holy Mother of God, and established for himself a monastery; and it was a refuge for Christians, a joy to the Angels, and perdition to the devil.

A.D. 1154. A.M. 6662. The men of Novgorod drove out *Knyaz* Yaroslav on March 26, and fetched in Rostislav, son of Mstislav, on April 17.

The same year they built a church to St. Sava.

The same year on November 14, Izyaslav died in Kiev. Then, too, Rostislav went from Novgorod to [take] the throne in Kiev, having left his son, David, in Novgorod. And the men of Novgorod were indignant, because he did not make order among them but tore them more apart; and they showed the road to his son after him. Then they sent *Vladyka* Nifont with the foremost men to Gyurgi for his son, and fetched in Mstislav, son of Gyurgi, on January 30. The same winter Vyacheslav died in Kiev.

Then, too, Rostislav went to Chernigov from Kiev, having sat in Kiev one week, and they defeated him, having deceived [him]; and Izyaslav Davidovits took his seat in Kiev.

A.D. 1155. A.M. 6663. In Palm week *Knyaz* Gyurgi entered Kiev and took his seat on the throne, and Izyaslav Davidovits fled to Chernigov; and Gyurgi received his nephews in peace with love, and distributed proper districts among them; and there was quiet in the Russian Land.

Chapter Five

FOREIGN OBSERVATIONS

*Many important details of life in Kievan Rus'
were recorded by foreign observers beginning in the ninth century. The three main
categories of this type of source material
through the thirteenth century are Latin
chronicles (primarily monastic), as well as accounts by visiting Latin-rite
ecclesiastics; Arabic and Farsi geographical literature; and Byzantine Greek
chronicles and governmental tracts. We have selected representative examples of each type of source for inclusion in this section.*

The first passage is an excerpt from the Chronicon *produced in the eleventh century by the German bishop of Meresberg, Ditmar. In the* Chronicon,
*a year-by-year account of important historical events, the passage entered
sub* anno *1018 contains a description of Kiev during the reign of Yaroslav
(in particular during his civil war with Mstislav). Ditmar notes that mercenaries were used within the Kievan military establishment, and that among
the mercenary force employed by the grand prince were foreign fugitives
and Danes. The translation is by Alexander Riasanovsky, from the Latin version of the* Chronicon *edited by F. Kurze which appears in the* Monumenta
Germaniae Historica, *SS t. 2 (Hanover 1889).*

*Some of the most important descriptions of the Rus' in medieval literature
appear in various versions of the* Kitāb al-Masālik wa 'l-Mamālik (Book of
Routes and Kingdoms). *Embellished and reproduced over and over again,
the* Kitāb al-Masālik wa 'l-Mamālik *was a literary genre produced by the
so-called Classical School of Islamic Geography. This school was not attached to any individual city, but was a tradition which flourished primarily
in the Islamic cities of Central Asia and the Tigris-Euphrates basin. The first
solid link in the Classical School of Islamic Geography is Ibn Khurdādhbih
(ca. 820–911), who served as the Director of Posts and Intelligence for the
Abbāsid Caliphate in the province of Jibāl and then as Director-General of
the same department in Baghdād and Sāmarra in the mid-ninth century. He
utilized the information which he acquired through the considerable intelligence networks of the caliphate, as well as tales of merchants and other
travellers to the Islamic lands and areas beyond the sphere of Islamic influence in his* Kitāb al-Masālik wa 'l-Mamālik. *The text is transmitted by William Watson from the Arabic edition of M. J. De Goejue (Leiden, 1889).*

Our third document in this section, De Administrando Imperio, *was compiled by the court of Byzantine emperor Constantine VII Porphyrogenitus (913–59) for the emperor's son (and himself a future emperor), Romanus II. Constantine actually met Princess Olga, the first ruler of Kievan Rus' to be baptized a Christian. It is said that Constantine fell in love with her and proposed marriage but that she, being loyal to her deceased husband Igor, skillfully deflected all such imperial advances. In addition to material on statecraft,* De administrando Imperio *includes a chapter on the northern neighbors of the Byzantine Empire (with advice on proper conduct with these "barbarians"). The English translation is by R. J.M H. Jenkins, from the Greek edition of Gy. Moravcsik.*

✤ *Ditmar of Merseberg's Description of Kiev[1]*

In this great city, which is the capital of this kingdom, there are held to be more than four-hundred churches and 8 markets, and moreover an undetermined number of people: which, like all the province, with the strength of runaway slaves coming together there from all parts and especially with the swift Danes resisted up to this point the Pechenegs who were inflicting injury on them and overcame others.

✤ *Ibn Khurdadhbih's Description of Rus Merchants[1]*

Following is an abbreviated gazetteer of terms used in the text:

The Rumi Sea (bahr ar-Rumi): The Black Sea (the term *bahr ar-Rum* was commonly used for the Mediterranean Sea).
The Tanis River: The Don River.
The Jurjan Sea: The Caspian Sea.
Wurut Tughuzghur: The Oghuz Turks.

They are a kind of as-Saqaliba and they trade furs, sables, and swords from the most distant (parts of the land) of as-Saqaliba to the Rumi Sea. The lord of ar-Rum levies taxes on them. When they go on the Tanis, the river

---

1. Reproduced by Alexander V. Riasanovsky, "Runaway Slaves' and 'Swift Danes' in Eleventh-Century Kiev," *Speculum* v. 39, no. 2 (April 1964), p. 291.

1. Note that as-Saqaliba is the Arabic word for "Slavs." Translated by William Watson from Ibn Khurdadhbih, *Kitab al-Masalik wa 'l-Mamalik,* ed. by M. J. De Goeje, *Bibliotheca Arabicorum Geographorum* (Leiden, 1889) pp. 54–55.

Photo: Icon of Saints Florus and Laurus, Novgorod School, Middle of the Sixteenth Century. This icon shows Persian influence.

of as-Saqāliba, they carry on through to Khamlīj, the city of the Khazars, and the lord of the Khazars collects tribute from them.

Then they come to the Jurjān Sea (Caspian) and disembark on its coast if they desire, which measures five hundred farsakhs. Sometimes they carry their goods from the Jurjān Sea by camelback to Baghdad. Saqāliba servants interpret for them. They claim that they are Christian, and that they are thus conveying the jizya.

When they go abroad, they go to al-Andalus or to Franja, then they go across to farthest Sūs, and then arrive in Tangier, then they go to Ifriqiyya, then to Egypt, then to Ramla, then to Damascus, then to Kufa, then to Baghdad, then to Basra, then to al-Ahwaz, then to Persia, then to Kirman, then to Sind, then to Hind, and then to China.

Sometimes they go in behind of ar-Rūm into the land of as-Saqāliba, then they go the Khamlij, the city of the Khazars, then to the Jurjān Sea, then to Balkh, then to Transoxiana, then to Wurut Tughuzghur, and then to China.

❖ *Constantine Porphyrogenitus' Description of Rus' and Their Ships*[1]

The 'monoxyla' which come down from outer Russia to Constantinople are from Novgorod, where Sviatoslav, son of Igor, prince of Russia, had his seat, and others from the city of Smolensk and from Teliutza and Chernigov and from Vyshegrad. All these come down the river Dnieper, and are collected together at the city of Kiev, also called Sambatas. Their Slav tributaries, the so-called Krivichians and the Lenzanenes and the rest of the Slavonic regions, cut the 'monoxyla' on their mountains in time of winter, and when they have prepared them, as spring approaches, and the ice melts, they bring them on to the neighbouring lakes. And since these *lakes* debouch into the river Dnieper, they enter thence on to this same river, and come down to Kiev, and draw *the ships* along to be finished and sell them to the Russians. The Russians buy these bottoms only, furnishing them with oars and rowlocks and other tackle from their old 'monoxyla', which they dismantle; *and so* they fit them out. And in the month of June they move off down the river Dnieper and come to Vitichev, which is a tributary city of the Russians, and there they gather during two or three days; and when all

---

1. Reprinted by permission of the publishers from G. Moravcsik (ed., Greek text), R. J. H. Jenkins (trans.) *Constantine Porphyrogenitus, De Administrando Imperio* (Washington, D.C., The Dumbarton Oaks Center for Byzantine Studies, 1967), pp. 57–63, alt.

the 'monoxyla' are collected together, then they set out, and come down the said Dnieper river. And first they come to the first barrage, called Essoupi, which means in Russian and Slavonic 'Do not sleep!'; the barrage itself is as narrow as the width of the Polo-ground; in the middle of it are rooted high rocks, which stand out like islands. Against these, then, comes the water and wells up and dashes down over the other side, with a mighty and terrific din. Therefore the Russians do not venture to pass between them, but put in to the bank hard by, disembarking the men on to dry land leaving the rest of the goods on board the 'monoxyla'; they then strip and, feeling with their feet to avoid striking on a rock, ***. This they do, some at the prow, some amidships, while others again, in the stern, punt with poles; and with all this careful procedure they pass this first barrage, edging round under the river-bank. When they have passed this barrage, they re-embark the others from the dry land and sail away, and come down to the second barrage, called in Russian Oulvorsi, and in Slavonic Ostrovouniprach, which means 'the Island of the Barrage'. This one is like the first, awkward and not to be passed through. Once again they disembark the men and convey the 'monoxyla' past, as on the first occasion. Similarly they pass the third barrage also, called Gelandri, which means in Slavonic 'Noise of the Barrage', and then the fourth barrage, the big one, called in Russian Aeifor, and in Slavonic Neasit, because the pelicans nest in the stones of the barrage. At this barrage all put into land prow foremost, and those who are deputed to keep the watch with them get out, and off they go, these men, and keep vigilant watch for the Pechenegs. The remainder, taking up the goods which they have on board the 'monoxyla', conduct the slaves in their chains past by land, six miles, until they are through the barrage. Then, partly dragging their 'monoxyla', partly portaging them on their shoulders, they convey them to the far side of the barrage; and then, putting them on the river and loading up their baggage, they embark themselves, and again sail off in them. When they come to the fifth barrage, called in Russian Varouforos, and in Slavonic Voulniprach, because it forms a large lake, they again convey their 'monoxyla' through at the edges of the river, as at the first and second barrages, and arrive at the sixth barrage, called in Russian Leanti, and in Slavonic Veroutzi, that is 'the Boiling of the Water', and this too they pass similarly. And thence they sail away to the seventh barrage, called in Russian Stroukoun, and in Slavonic Naprezi, which means 'Little Barrage'. This they pass at the so-called ford of *Vrar,* where the Chersonites cross over from Russia and the Pechenegs to Cherson; which ford is as wide as the Hippodrome, and, measured upstream from the bottom as far as the rocks break surface, a bow-shot in length. It is at this point, therefore, that the Pechenegs come down and attack the Russians. After traversing this place, they reach the island called St. Gregory, on which island they perform their sacrifices because a gigantic oak-tree stands there; and they sacrifice live cocks. Arrows, too, they peg in round about, and others bread and meat, or something of whatever each may have, as is their custom. They also throw lots regarding the cocks, whether to slaughter them, or to eat them as well, or to leave them alive. From this island onwards the Russians do not fear the Pecheneg until they reach the river Selinas. So then they start off thence and sail for four days, until they reach the lake which forms the mouth of the river, on which is the island of St. Aitherios. Arrived at this island, they rest themselves there for two or three days. And they re-equip their 'monoxyla' with such tackle as is needed, sails and masts and rudders, which they bring with them. Since this lake is the mouth of this river, as has been said, and carries on down to the sea, and the island of St. Aitherios lies on the sea, they come thence to the Dniester river, and having got safely there they rest again. But when the weather is propitious, they put to sea and come to the river called Aspros, and after resting there too in like manner, they again set out and come to the Selinas, to the so-called branch of the Danube river. And until they are past the river Selinas, the Pechenegs keep pace with them. And if it happens that the sea casts a ''monoxylon' on shore, they all put in to land, in order to present a united opposition to the Pechenegs. But after the Selinas they fear nobody, but, entering the territory of Bulgaria, they come to the mouth of the Danube. From the Danube they proceed to the Konopas, and from the Konopas to Constantia, *and from Constantia* to the river of Varna, and from Varna they come to the river Ditzina, all of which are Bulgarian territory. From the Ditzina they reach the district of Mesembria, and there at last their voyage, fraught with such travail and terror, such difficulty and danger, is at an end. The severe manner of life of these same Russians in winter-time is as follows. When the month of November begins, their chiefs together with all the Russians at once leave Kiev and go off on the 'poliudia', which means 'rounds', that is, to the Slavonic regions of the Vervians and Drugovichians and Krivichians and Severians and the rest of the Slavs who are tributaries of the Russians. There they are maintained throughout the winter, but then once more, starting from the month of April, when the ice of the Dnieper river melts, they come back to Kiev. They then pick up their 'monoxyla', as has been said above, and fit them out, and come down to Romania.

Bibliography

The earliest period of Russian history has traditionally posed the most problematic and controversial questions in Russian historiography (such the Normanist/Anti-Normanist Controversy). Consequently, theories are frequently revised and books once considered to be seminal are discarded by a new generation of scholars. The three following books, however, are recommended because of their scholarly longevity and are widely considered to be standard texts for the early period of Russian history:

Nicholas V. Riasanovsky, *A History of Russia* (fourth edition; New York and Oxford, 1984). Chapters one, two and three concern the Kievan period.

George Vernadsky, *Ancient Russia* (New Haven, 1943). *Idem, Kievan Russia* (New Haven, 1948).

For the conversion of Russia to Christianity, see in particular Albert Leong, ed., *The Millennium: Christianity and Russia, 988–1988* (Crestwood, N.Y., 1990).

From among the many articles reflecting recent trends in historical and archaeological research for the early period of Russian history, see the following:

Alexander V. Riasanovsky, "The Varangian Question," in *I Normanni e la loro espansione in Europea nell'alto medioevo, Settimane di studio del centro Italiano di studi sull'alto medioevo* 16 (Spoleto, 1969).

Idem, "The Embassy, of 838 Revisited: Some Comments in Connection with a 'Normanist' Source on Early Russian History," in *Jahrbücher für Geschichte Osteuropas* (Wiesbaden, 1962).

Jonathan Shepard, "Some Problems of Russo-Byzantine Relations, c. 860–1050," in *The Slavonic and East European Review* 52 (1974).

Idem, "The Russian Steppe-Frontier and the Black Sea Zone," in *Archeion Pontou* 35 (1979).

Thomas S. Noonan, "When and How Dirhams First Reached Russia," in *Cahiers du Monde russe at sovietique* 21 (1980).

Idem, "Monetary Circulation Early Medieval Rus': A study of Volga Bulgar Dirham Finds," in *Russian History/Histoire Russe* 7, pt. 3, (1980).

Questions to Consider

1. Considering the information contained in *The Primary Chronicle* and in the work of foreign observers such as Ibn *Kh*urda*dh*bih and Constantine Porphyrogenitus, what were the primary occupations of the early Rus'?

2. What was the significance of plunder and tribute in the economy of Kievan Rus'?

3. What are the reasons given in *The Primary Chronicle* for the decision of Vladimir to convert to Eastern Orthodox Christianity?

4. What elements of Byzantine Greek religious culture were adopted by the Rus'?

5. What does Yaroslav's *Russkaya Pravda* reveal about the social structure of Kievan Rus'?

6. What kind of hardships did the inhabitants of medieval Russia face on a daily basis, as revealed in *The Novgorod Chronicle?*

7. Although Kiev and Novgorod were bound together politically, how did Novgorod's municipal government differ from that of kiev?

8. What kinds of political problems weakened Kievan Rus' before the advent of the Mongol/Tatar Yoke?

PART TWO

The Tatar Yoke

Chapter Six

THE INVASION OF RUSSIA

Sedentary civilization in Russia was threatened by the influx of nomadic Asiatic tribes from circa 1000 B.C., when the Cimmerians invaded the steppe region, until the fifteenth century, when the Tatar domination of Russian cities was finally ended. Of the many Asiatic invasions of Russia, that of the Tatars was the most destructive. Initially, an army commanded by the Mongol leader Subadai defeated a combined force of Russians and Polovtsi (Cumans) in 1223 on the Kalka river, near the Sea of Azov. Although the invaders suddenly withdrew after this victory owing to the unstable political situation in Mongolia, Batu Khan and his military commander Subadai returned fourteen years later leading a tribal alliance of the Blue and Silver Hordes, known as the Golden Horde. Despite the fact that the leadership of the army was Mongol, two-thirds to three-quarters of the force was non-Mongol, including Turkic horsemen and Chinese engineers. The Russians collectively referred to these invaders as Tatars, but the Tatars were actually only the tribe which performed the function of advancing before the main Mongol force as shock troops.

Demanding tribute from the terrified princes of central and northern Russia, the Tatars ventured out of Sarai, their regional capital on the Volga, to demolish those Russian cities which refused to submit to the Great Khan. Many central and northern princes voluntarily submitted to the Tatars, saving their cities by paying an annual tribute. "Eurasianist" historians have argued that the Tatars affected later political and economic developments in Russia as a result of cross-cultural contacts which occurred during the years of the Tatar Yoke, and that Russia became a homogenized amalgam of East and West. Other historians have argued that Tatar influence in Russia was relatively minor due to the fact that the Golden Horde was more interested in gathering tribute from the Russian princes than with settling down (and the Orthodox Church discouraged both intermarriage and the sending of missions among the few Tatars who resided on the southern steppe).

Our first two selections in this section are excerpts from medieval chronicles describing the Tatar capture of several cities in northern Russia in 1237–38 and the Tatar conquest of Kiev in 1240, translated by Basil Dmytryshyn. The third passage in this section, taken from The Secret History of the Mongols, *describes the conquest of Russia from the Mongol perspective. Although the original Mongol text has not survived, it was translated into Chinese by the Ming court in 1382, and has been translated into English by Francis Woodman Cleaves.*

✦ *The Tatar Conquest of Northern Rus' Cities*[1]

It happened in 1237. That winter, the godless Tatars, under the leadership of Batu, came to the Riazan principality from the East through the forests. Upon arriving they encamped at Onuza, which they took and burned. From here they dispatched their emissaries—a woman witch and two men—to the princes of Riazan demanding a tithe from the princes and complete armor and horses from the people. The princes of Riazan, Iurii Igorevich and his brother Oleg, did not allow the emissaries to enter the city, and [together with] the Murom and Pronsk princes [they] moved against the Tatars in the direction of Voronezh. The princes replied: "When we are gone, everything will be yours." . . . The princes of Riazan sent a plea to Prince Iurii of Vladimir, begging him to send aid or to come in person. Prince Iurii, however, did not go; neither did he listen to the plea of the princes of Riazan, as he wanted to fight the Tatars alone. . . .

The princes of Riazan, Murom, and Pronsk moved against the godless and engaged them in a battle. The struggle was fierce, but the godless Mohammedans emerged victorious with each prince fleeing toward his own city. Thus angered, the Tatars now began the conquest of the Riazan land with great fury. They destroyed cities, killed people, burned, and took [people] into slavery. On December 6, [1237] the cursed strangers approached the capital city of Riazan, besieged it, and surrounded it with a stockade. The princes of Riazan shut themselves up with the people of the city, fought bravely, but succumbed. On December 21, [1237] the Tatars took the city of Riazan, burned it completely, killed Prince Iurii Igorevich, his wife, slaughtered other princes, and of the captured men, women, and children, some they killed with their swords, others they killed with arrows and [then] threw them into the fire; while some of the captured they bound, cut, and disemboweled their bodies. The Tatars burned many holy churches, monasteries, and villages, and took their property.

Then the Tatars went toward Kolomna. From Vladimir, Grand Prince Iurii Vsevolodovich sent his son, Prince Vsevolod, against them; with him also went Prince Roman Igorevich of Riazan with his armies. Grand Prince Iurii sent his military commander, Eremei Glebovich, ahead with a patrol. This

---

1Reprinted by permission of the publishers from Basil Dmytryshyn (ed. and trans.), *Medieval Russia: A Source Book, 850–1700* (New York, Holt, Rinehart, and Winston, 1990), pp. 146–49.

Photo: Icon of the battle between Yaroslav and Svyatopolk the Accused, from the Life of Boris and Gleb. Late Sixteenth Century.

group joined Vsevolod's and Roman Igorevich's forces at Kolomna. There they were surrounded by the Tatars. The struggle was very fierce and the Russians were driven away to a hill. And there they [the Tatars] killed Prince Roman Igorevich Riazanskii, and Eremei Glebovich, the military commander of Vsevolod Iurievich, and they slaughtered many other men. Prince Vsevolod, with a small detachment, fled to Vladimir. The Tatars [then] went toward Moscow. They took Moscow and killed the military commander Philip Nianka, and captured Vladimir, the son of Prince Iurii; they slaughtered people old and young alike, some they took with them into captivity; they departed with a great amount of wealth.

When Grand Prince Iurii Vsevolodovich heard about this . . . he entrusted the rule of Vladimir to a bishop, Princes Vsevolod and Mstislav, and his own military leader Peter Osliadiukovich, while he himself went toward the Volga with his nephews—Vasilko Konstantinovich, Vsevolod Konstanti-novich, and Vladimir Konstantinovich. They made their camp on the Siti. There the Grand Prince awaited the arrival of his brothers—Prince Iaroslav Vsevolodovich and Prince Sviatoslav Vsevolodovich—with their soldiers, and he himself began to collect an army; while he appointed Zhiroslav Mik-hailovich his military commander.

On Tuesday February 3, [1238] . . . the Tatars approached Vladimir. The inhabitants of Vladimir, with their princes and military commander, Peter Osliadiukovich, shut themselves up in the city. The Tatars came to the Gold-en Gates, brought with them Prince Vladimir, the son of the Grand Prince Iurii Vsevolodovich, and inquired: "Is the Grand Prince Iurii in the city?" But the inhabitants of Vladimir began to shoot at them. They, however, shouted: "Do not shoot!" And, having approached very close to the gates, they showed the inhabitants of Vladimir their young Prince Vladimir, son of Iurii, and asked: "Do you recognize your young Prince?" As a result of privation and misfortune, his face was sad and he looked weak. Vsevolod and Mstislav stood atop the Golden Gates and recognized their brother Vladimir. Oh, how sad and tearful it is to see one's brother in such a condi-tion! Vsevolod and Mstislav, with their *boyars* and all the inhabitants, wept as they looked at Vladimir. And the Tatars departed from the Golden Gates, circled the entire city, examined it, and encamped at Zremany in front of the Golden Gates and about the entire city; and there were many of them. . . .

After they made camp around Vladimir, the Tatars went and occupied the city of Suzdal. . . . They brought a multitude of prisoners into their camp, approached the city of Vladimir on Saturday, and from early morning till evening they built scaffolds and set up rams, and during the night they sur-rounded the entire city with a fence. In the morning, the princes, Bishop Mitrophan, military leader Peter Osliadiukovich, and all the *boyars* and the people realized that their city would be taken and they all began to weep. . . . On Sunday, February 8, [1238] . . . early in the morning the Tatars ap-proached the city from all sides and began to hit the city [walls] with rams, and began to pour great stones into the center of the city from far away, as if by God's will, as if it rained inside the city; many people were killed inside the city and all were greatly frightened and trembled. The Tatars broke through the wall at the Golden Gates, also from the Lybed [side] at the Orininy and the Copper Gates, and from the Kliazma [direction] at the Volga Gates, and in other places; they destroyed the whole city, threw stones inside, and . . . entered it from all sides like demons. Before dinner they took the new city which they set on fire; and there they killed Prince Vsevolod with his brother, many *boyars* and people, while other princes and all the people fled into the middle city. Bishop Mitrophan and the Grand Duchess with her sons and daughters, daughters-in-law, grandchildren, *boyars,* and their wives, and many people fled into a church, locked the church gates, and climbed inside the church to the choir loft. The Tatars took this city too, and began to search after the princes and their mother, and found that they were inside the church. . . . The Tatars broke the gates of the church and slaughtered those who were inside and resisted. And they began to ask the whereabouts of the princes and their mother and found they were in the choir loft. They began to entice them to come down. But they did not listen to them. The Tatars then brought many fire logs inside the church and set it on fire. Those present in the choir loft, praying, gave their souls to God; they were burned and joined the list of martyrs. And the Tatars pillaged the holy church, and they tore the miracle-making icon of the Mother of God.

From here the Tatars advanced against Grand Prince Iurii; some went toward Rostov, while others went toward Iaroslavl, which they took; some went along the Volga and toward Gorodets and burned everything along the Volga up to Merski Golich. Some went toward Pereiaslavl and took that city and slaughtered the people. And from there they set the entire countryside and many cities on fire: Iuriev, Dmitrov, Volok, Tver, where they also killed Iaroslav's son; and there was not a town till Torzhok which was not occupied by the Tatars. In February [1238], in the Rostov and Suzdal principalities alone, they took fourteen cities in addition to villages and churchyards.

At the end of February [1238], a messenger brought the news to Grand Prince Iurii Vsevolodovich, his brother Sviatoslav Vsevolodovich, and their nephews Vasilko, Vsevolod, and Vladimir Konstantinovich, that the city of Vladimir had been captured, the bishop, grand dukes, princes, and all the inhabitants had been burned and some slaughtered. "And they killed your eldest son Vsevolod, and his brothers, inside the city and now they go toward you." . . . Iurii waited for his brother Iaroslav, but he did not come. And the prince ordered that his military leader strengthen his people and prepare them to fight, and sent a brave man, Dorofei Semeonovich, with 3000 men, to gather information about the Tatars. But hardly had he left when he returned with these words: "Lord! The Tatars have surrounded us."

When he heard this, Prince Iurii with his brother Sviatoslav and his nephews—Vasilko, Vsevolod, and Vladimir—and with their men, mounted their horses and advanced against the heathens. Grand Prince Iurii Vsevolodovich began to organize his regiments when suddenly the Tatars arrived at Siti. Prince Iruii forgot all about fear and advanced to meet them. Regiments met and there ensued a major battle and fierce slaughter; blood flowed like water. Because of God's will, the Tatars defeated the Russian princes. Grand Prince of Vladimir, Iurii Vsevolodovich, was killed then as were many of his military leaders and *boyars* and soldiers. The Tatars took his nephew, Vasilko Konstantinovich of Rostrov, into captivity and brought him to the Sherenskii Forest. They also encamped there.

✤ *The Tatar Conquest of Kiev*[1]

In this year [1240] Batu Khan approached and surrounded the city of Kiev with a great multitude of soldiers. The Tatar force besieged it and it was impossible for any one either to leave the city or to enter it. Squeaking of wagons, bellowing of camels, sounds of trumpets and organs, neighing of horses, and cry and sobs of an innumerable multitude of people made it impossible to hear one another in the city. The entire country was overflowing with Tatars. The Kievans then captured a Tatar by the name of Tavrul, and he named all the great princes who were with Batu, and spoke of his innumerable strength. And he had with him the following of his brothers and of his strong military leaders: Urdiuy, Baydar, Biriuy, Kaydar, Bechar, Mengay, Kailug, [and] Kuiuk; but he [Kuiuk] returned [to Mongolia] when he learned of the death of the [Great] Khan. [The Great] Khan did not belong to the Batu family, but was his first and great leader. Batu Khan mourned him because the latter liked him very much. Other military leaders [of Batu Khan at Kiev] and great princes included: Butar, Aydar, Kilemet, Burunday, Batyr, who captured the Bulgar and Suzdal lands, and a great number, countless, other military leaders. Batu ordered that many wall-destroying rams be brought to Kiev and placed near the Polish Gate, because that part was wooded. Many rams hammered the walls without interruption day and night and the inhabitants were frightened, and there were many killed and blood flowed like water. And Batu sent the following message to the inhabitants of Kiev: "If you surrender to me, you will be forgiven; if, however, you are going to resist you will suffer greatly and will perish cruelly." The inhabitants of Kiev, however, did not listen to him, but calumniated and cursed him. This angered Batu very much and he ordered [his men] to attack the city with great fury. And thus with the aid of many rams they broke through the city walls and entered the city, and the inhabitants ran to meet

---

1. Reprinted by permission of the publishers from Basil Dmytryshyn (ed. and trans.), Medieval Russia: A Source Book, 850–1700 (New York, Holt, Rinehart, and Winston, 1990), pp. 151–52.

them. It was possible to hear and see a great crash of lances and clatter of shields; the arrows obscured the light and because of this it was impossible to see the sky, but there was darkness from the multitude of Tatar arrows, and there were dead everywhere and everywhere blood flowed like water. [Kiev's] military leader Dmitrii was severely wounded and many strong men were killed. The inhabitants [of Kiev] were defeated, and the Tatars climbed on the walls and because of great exhaustion they remained there. The night came. During the night the inhabitants [of Kiev] built a new fortification around the Church of the Virgin Mary. When morning came the Tatars attacked them and there was a bitter slaughter. Some people fainted and [some] fled to the church steeple with their possessions; and the church walls collapsed from the weight and the Tatars took the city of Kiev on St. Nicholas Day, December 6, [1240]. They brought the wounded military leader Dmitrii before Batu, and Batu ordered that he not be killed because of his bravery. And Batu began to inquire about Prince Daniel [of Galicia], and they told him that the Prince had fled to Hungary. Batu left his own military leader in Kiev and he himself went toward Vladimir in Volyn.

✜ *The Conquest of the Rus' According to the Mongols[1]*

Again he made Sübe'etei Ba'atur to go a warfare northward unto these eleven tribes of realms and peoples: Qanglin, Kibča'ud, Bajigid, Orusud, Majarad, Asud, Sasud, Serkesüd, Kesimir, Bolar, and Kerel and, making [him] to cross the Idil and the Jayay rivers full of water, [he made] Sube'etei Ba'atur [to go a warfare] unto the city of Kiwa Menkermen.

The many princes having at their head Batu, Büri, Güyüg, and Möngge which had gone a warfare, the succourers of Sübe'etei Ba'atur, causing the Qanglin, the Kibca'ud, and the Bajigid to submit themselves, [passing over] the Ejil and the Jayay [rivers] and breaking the city of Meged, slaying the

1Note that Orsud is the Mongol word for the people of Russia; Kiwa Menkerme (or just Kiwa) is Kiev; the Idil is the Volga; and the Jayay is the Ural. Reprinted by permission of the publishers and the editor/translater from Francis Woodman Cleaves (ed. and trans.), *The Secret History of the Mongols* (Cambridge, Mass., Harvard University Press and the Harvard, Yenching Institute, 1982), v. 1, pp. 203, 214–215, 218–219.

Orusud, spoiled till they destroyed [them]. Spoiling and making the people of the cities having at their head Asud, Sesüd, Bolar, Mankerman, and Kiwa, placing *daruyacin and tammacin,* they returned. He made to go a warfare Yesüder Qorci, the succourer of Jalayirtai Qorci which aforetime had gone a warfare against the Jürced and the Solangyas. He made a decree, saying, "Let him sit [there] as *tamma.*"

When Batu, from on the Kibčay warfare, petitioned, by messengers, unto Ögödei Qahan, he sent, petitioning, saying "In the night of Everlasting Heaven and in the fortune of [mine] uncle the Qahan, breaking the city of Meged, spoiling the Orusud people, making to submit themselves in an upright manner eleven realms of people, withdrawing ourselves, pulling the 'golden reins,' saying unto one another, 'Let us feast a feast at which we shall separate ourselves from one another,' pitching a great tent.

Art thou looking upon the Orusud people as having submitted themselves, fearing for [cause of] that thy fury and wrath? Thinking like as [thou] by [thyself] alone hadst brought the Orusud people into subjection, taking in hand [thine] heart of violence, goest thou forward, rebelling against the person [which is thine] elder brother? It was in the decree of Our father Činggis Qahan. Was he not wont to say,

> 'A multitude causeth [one] to be afraid.
> A depth causeth [one] to die'?

Like as [thou] hadst accomplished [it] by [thyself] alone, going in the shelter of both Sübe'etei and Büjeg, joining thyself by the multitude and by all, bringing into subjection the Orusud and the Kibča'ud, getting one or two Orusud and Kibča'ud, at the moment when [thou] hadst not yet gotten and gathered the lower leg of a kid, presuming on [thy] manliness, issuing [but] once from in the tent, like as [thou] hadst accomplished even aught by [thyself] alone, provoking words, thou [art] coming. By Menggei, Alcidai, Qongqortai, Janggi and others,

> Letting—[they] being companions [always] at hand—to restrain
> [Our] heart which was risen;
> Letting—[they] being broad spoons—to be caused to pacify
> The kettle which boileth.[1]

1This was addressed to Ogedei, the Great Khan, by several Mongol princes.

CHAPTER SEVEN

THE AFTERMATH

Although some of the central and northern Russian cities such as Riazan, Suzdal, and Vladimir were attacked by the Tatars in 1237–38, the Golden Horde never intended to occupy the northern forest, where their cavalry would be less effective than on the open plains in the south. The objective of the Tatar armies in 1237–38 had not been to simply instill a fear of their warriors in the northern forest area, but to isolate Kiev and protect their flank in preparation for their impending advance on that city. The demographics of the southeastern steppe changed drastically because of the Tatar policy of deporting Kievan citizens to Asia, as well as the periodic massacres that attended the crushing of rebellions, and the northern migrations of boyars and peasants in search of land and safety. Thus, central and northern cities became the political, economic, and cultural centers of Russia, while the south was for centuries an underpopulated and economically stagnant region.

The great northern city of Novgorod flourished in the absence of a strong rival in Kiev, but even the greatest of Novgorod's princes, Alexander Nevsky (1252–63), who had earlier won decisive victories over the Swedes on the Neva river (1240) and the Teutonic Knights on the frozen ice of Lake Peipus (1242), was forced to submit to the Great Khan in person, travelling to the distant Mongol capital of Karakorum. The city of Moscow grew in importance in this period. A century after its appearance as a small but strategically-located fort on the Moscva river, Alexander Nevsky acquired possession of the city and created a principality there for his youngest son Daniil (1276–1303).

Before the Tatar Yoke, tribal differentiations coalesced into regional differentiations, but a degree of cultural unity existed in Russia, in the form of a common religion and a common scholarly (and quite probably spoken) language. Under the Grand Princes in Kiev, a degree of political unity existed, as well. After the Tatar conquest, however, Russia, Belorussia, and the Ukraine became articulated as separate national entities.

The first passage in this section is taken from the account of the journey of Friar John of Pian de Carpine to Mongolia at the behest of Pope Innocent IV in 1245–47. This was the era of the crusades, and the Latin West was increasingly interested in the Mongol Empire as a potential ally in its perennial struggle with the Islamic world. Setting out from Lyon with an epistle from Innocent IV which inquired whether the great khan would be interested in receiving Roman Catholic missions into his empire, Friar John passed through Russia on his way to Karakorum. The text is translated from the Latin by William Woodville Rockhill.

Our second passage consists of excerpts from The Novgorod Chronicle, sub annis *1258–1261, which describe the relationship of Novgorod to the Tatars (translated by Michell and Forbes). The third passage consists of the entries in* The Novgorod Chronicle, sub annis *1262–63, which refer to the journey of Alexander Nevsky to Mongolia and his subsequent death (translated by Michell and Forbes).*

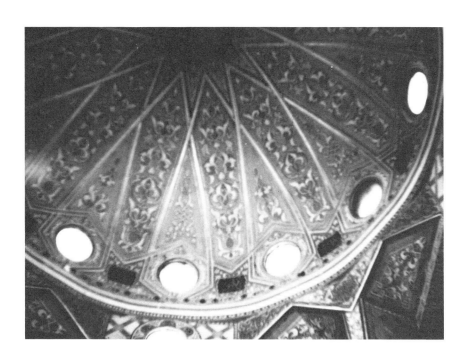

⬥ The Journey of Friar John of Pian de Carpine[1]

The latter also gave us his letters and an escort and money for our expenses in his towns and cities, as far as Conrad, Duke of Lenczy. At that time, through God's special grace, the Lord Vassilko, Duke of Ruscia, had come there, from whom we learnt more accurately of the Tartars: for he had sent his ambassadors to them, who had come back to him and to his brother Daniel, bearing to the lord Daniel a safe conduct to go to Bati. And he told us that if we wanted to go to them we must have rich presents to give them, for they were in the habit of asking for them most importunately, and if they were not given them (and this is quite true), an ambassador could not conduct his business satisfactorily with them; and that furthermore he was looked upon as a mere nothing. Not wishing that the affairs of the Lord Pope and of the Church should be obstructed on this account, with some of that which had been given us in charity, so that we should not be in want and for use on our journey, we bought some skins of beavers and of some other animals. Duke Conrad, the Duchess of Cracow, some knights and the bishop of Cracow, hearing of this, gave us some more of these skins. Furthermore Duke Conrad, his son, and the Bishop of Cracow besought most earnestly Duke Vassilko to help us as much as he could in reaching the Tartars; and he replied that he would do so willingly.

So he took us with him to his country; and as he kept us for some days as his guests that we might rest a little, and had called thither his bishops at our request, we read them the letters of the Lord Pope, in which he admonished them to return to the unity of holy mother Church; we also advised and urged them as much as we could, as well the Duke as the Bishops, and all those who had met there, to that same end. But as at the very time when this duke had come to Poland, his brother, Duke Daniel, had gone to Bati and was not present, they could not give a final answer, but must wait his return before being able to give a full reply.

After that the Duke sent one of his servants with us as far as Kiew. Nevertheless we travelled ever in danger of our lives on account of the

---

1. This passage begins with the receipt by Friar John of support from the Duke of Silesia, Boleslas, for his journey further into Eastern Europe. The passage is reprinted by permission of the publishers from William Woodville Rockhill (ed. and trans.), *The Journey of William of Rubruck to the Eastern Parts of the World, 1253–55* (London, the Hakluyt Society, 1900), pp. 2–4; 10, 12, 20, 25–27; 31–32.

Photo: Domed interior of a mosque in Russia.

Lithuanians, who often committed undiscovered outrages as much as possible in the country of Ruscia, and particularly in these places through which we had to pass; and as the greater part of the men of Ruscia had been killed by the Tartars or taken off into captivity, they were unable to offer them the least resistance; we were safe, however, from the Ruthenians on account of this servant. Thence then, by the grace of God having been saved from the enemies of the Cross of Christ, we came to Kiew, which is the metropolis of Ruscia. And when we came there we took counsel with the Millenarius, and the other nobles who were there, as to our route. They told us that if we took into Tartary the horses which we had, they would all die, for the snows were deep, and they did not know how to dig out the grass from under the snow like Tartar horses, nor could anything else be found (on the way) for them to eat, for the Tartars had neither straw nor hay nor fodder. So, on their advice, we decided to leave our horses there with two servants to keep them; and we had to give the Millenarius presents, that he might be pleased to give us pack-horses and an escort. Before we reached Kiew, when in Danilov, I was ill to the point of death; but I had myself carried along in a cart in the intense cold through the deep snow, so as not to interfere with the affairs of Christendom.

Having settled then all these matters at Kiew, on the second day after the feast of the Purification of Our Lady (February 4, 1246), we started out from Kiew for other barbarous peoples, with the horses of the Millenarius and an escort. We came to a certain town which was under the direct rule of the Tartars and is called Canov; the prefect of the town gave us horses and an escort as far as another town in which was a certain Alan prefect who was called Micheas, a man full of all malice and iniquity, for he had sent to us to Kiew some of his body-guard, who lyingly said to us, as from the part of Corenza, that we being ambassadors were to come to him; and this he did, though it was not true, in order that he might extort presents from us. When, however, we reached him, he made himself most disagreeable, and unless we promised him presents, would in no wise agree to help us. Seeing that we would not otherwise be able to go farther, we promised to give him some presents, but when we gave him what appeared to us suitable, he refused to receive them unless we gave more; and so we had to add to them according to his will, and something besides he subtracted from us deceitfully and maliciously.

They called us inside (the tent), and gave us mead, for we would not drink mare's milk at all; and this was a great honor they showed us; and they kept on urging us to drink, but not being in the habit of it, we could not do so, and we let them see that it was distasteful to us, so they stopped pressing us. In the great square was the duke Jeroslav of Susdal in Ruscia, and several princes of the Kitayans and Solanges, also two sons of the King of Georgia, a soldan, the ambassador of the Calif of Baldach, and more than ten other soldans of the Saracens, I believe, and as we were told by the procurators. For there were more than four thousand envoys, as well those bringing tribute as those offering presents, soldans and other chiefs who had come to present themselves in person, those who had been sent by their (rulers), and those who were governors of countries. All these were put together outside the paling, and drink was given to them at the same time; as for ourselves and the duke Jeroslav, whenever we were outside with them they always gave us a higher place.

At this same time Jeroslav, grand-duke in a part of Ruscia called Susdal, died at the Emperor's *orda*. It happened that he was invited by the mother of the Emperor (to her tent), and she gave him to eat and drink with her own hand, as if to honour him; and he went back to his lodgings straightway and fell ill, and after seven days he was dead, and all his body became livid in strange fashion; so that everyone believed that he had been poisoned, that they might get free and full possession of his lands. As an argument in favour of this (supposition, the Empress) sent at once, without the knowledge of any of her people who were there, an envoy in all haste to his son Alexander in Ruscia to come to her, for she wished to give him his father's lands; but he would not go, but remained there (at home); in the meanwhile (the Empress) sent also letters for him to come and receive his father's lands. It was believed by all that he would be put to death if he should come, or imprisoned perpetually.

It was after this death (of Jeroslav) that our Tartars took us to the Emperor, if I remember correctly the time; and when the Emperor heard from our Tartars that we had come to him, he ordered us to go back to his mother, for he wanted two days after that to unfurl his standard against the whole of the western world, as was emphatically told us by those who knew, as has been previously stated, and he wished us not to know it. When we had returned (to the Empress), we remained there a few days, when we were sent back again to him; and we remained with him for quite a month, in such hunger and thirst that we were barely able to keep alive, for the allowances which they gave the four of us were scarcely enough for one; and we could find nothing to buy, the market being too far away. Had not the Lord sent us a certain Ruthenian called Cosmas, a goldsmith, and a great favourite of the Emperor, who helped us a little, I verily believe we should have died, unless the Lord had helped us in some other way. He showed us before putting it in place the throne of the Emperor which he himself had made, and also the seal he had manufactured for him, and he told us the superscription on his seal. We also learnt many private details (*secreta*) about the Emperor, from those who had come with other chiefs, several Ruthenians and Hungarians who knew Latin and French, also Ruthenian clerks and others who had been with them, some as long as thirty years, in war and in other events, and who knew all about them as they understood the language, having been continually with them some twenty, others ten years, more or less. From these we were able to learn about everything: they told us most freely of all things without our having to question them, for they knew of our desire.

After these things had happened the Emperor sent his prothonotary Chingay to tell us to write down what we had to say and our business, and to give it to him; this we did, writing down all we had previously said at Bati's, as has been stated above. After an interval of several days, he had us again called, and told us, through Kadac, the procurator of the whole empire, and in the presence of the prothonotaries Bala and Chingay, and of many others of his secretaries, to say all we had to say; and this we did right willingly. Our interpreter on that occasion, as well as on the other, was Temer, a knight of Jeroslav's, now a clerk with him, and another clerk of the Emperor's.

✣ *Novgorod and the Tatars*[1]

A.D. 1258. A.M. 6766. The Lithuanians with the men of Polotsk came to Smolensk and took [the town of] Voishchina by assault. The same autumn the Lithuanians came to Torzhok, and the men of Novi-torg issued out. For our sins the Lithuanians ambushed them; some they killed, others they took with their hands, and others barely escaped; and there was much evil in Torzhok. The same winter the Tartars took the whole Lithuanian land, and killed the people.

A.D. 1259. A.M. 6767. There was a sign in the moon; such as no sign had ever been. The same winter Mikhail Pineschinich came from the Low Country with a false mission, saying thus: "If you do not number yourselves for tribute there is already a force in the Low Country." And the men of Novgorod did number themselves for tribute. The same winter the accursed raw-eating Tartars, Berkai and Kasachik, came with their wives, and many others, and there was a great tumult in Novgorod, and they did much evil in the province, taking contribution for the accursed Tartars. And the accursed ones began to fear death; they said to Olexander: "Give us guards, lest they kill us." And the *Knyaz* ordered the son of the *Posadnik* and all the sons of the *Boyars* to protect them by night. The Tartars said: "Give us your numbers for tribute or we will run away." And the common people would not give

---

1. Reprinted by permission of the publishers from Robert Michell and Nevill Forbes (eds. and trans.), *The Novgorod Chronicle,* 1016–1471 (Gulf Breeze, Florida, Academic International Press, 1970), pp. 96–97. Note that Olexander is a variant of Alexander.

their numbers for tribute but said: "Let us die honourably for St. Sophia and for the angelic houses." Then the people were divided: who was good stood by St. Sophia and by the True Faith; and they made opposition; the greater men bade the lesser be counted for tribute. And the accursed ones wanted to escape, driven by the Holy Spirit, and they devised an evil counsel how to strike at the town at the other side, and the others at this side by the lake; and Christ's power evidently forbade them, and they durst not. And becoming frightened they began to crowd to one point to St. Sophia, saying: "Let us lay our heads by St. Sophia." And it was on the morrow, the *Knyaz* rode down from the *Gorodische* and the accursed Tartars with him, and by the counsel of the evil they numbered themselves for tribute; for the *Boyars* thought it would be easy for themselves, but fall hard on the lesser men. And the accursed ones began to ride through the streets, writing down the Christian houses; because for our sins God has brought wild beasts out of the desert to eat the flesh of the strong, and to drink the blood of *Boyars*. And having numbered them for tribute and taken it, the accursed ones went away, and *Knyaz* Olexander followed them, having set his son Dmitri on the throne.

The same year, on the eve of Boris Day, there was a great frost throughout the province; but the Lord did not wish to leave this place of St. Sophia waste. He turned away His wrath from us and looked down on us with the eye of His mercy, pointing us to repentance; but we sinners return like dogs to our vomit, unmindful of God's punishments which come upon us for our sins.

A.D. 1260. A.M. 6768. There was quiet all the year.

A.D. 1261. A.M. 6769. *Vladyka* Dalmat of Novgorod covered the whole roof of St. Sophia with lead. The same year, on November 8, the Feast of St. Michael, the Church of St. Vasili and thirty big houses were burnt down, and on the morrow the Church of St. Dmitri in Slavkov Street was burnt down, and fifty big houses.

✛ *The Death of Alexander Nevsky[1]*

The same year (1262) *Knyaz* Olexander went to the Tartars; and Berka kept him, not letting him back to Russia; and he wintered with the Tartars and fell ill.

---

1. Reprinted by permission of the publishers from Robert Michell and Nevill Forbes (eds. and trans.), *The Novgorod Chronicle, 1016–1471* (Gulf Breeze, Florida, Academic International Press, 1970), p. 98.

A.D. 1263. A.M. 6771. *Knyaz* Olexander came back from the Tartars in very bad health, in the autumn; and he came to Gorodets [monastery] and was shorn on November 14, the day of the holy Apostle Philip; and he died the same night and they took him to Volodimir and laid him in the monastery of the Nativity by the Church of the Holy Mother of God. And the Bishops and *Igumens* having come together with the Metropolitan Kyuril and all the hierarchy and monks and with all the people of Suzdal, they buried him honourably on the 23rd of the same month, Friday, the Day of St. Amfilokhi. Grant him, O merciful Lord, to see Thy face in the future age, for he laboured for Novgorod and for all the Russian land.

Bibliography

From the vast literature on the Tatars and Russia, see in particular the following works:

Christopher Dawson, ed., *Mission to Asia: Narratives and Letters of the Franciscan Missionaries in Mongolia and China in the Thirteenth and Fourteenth Centuries* (New York, 1966).

Charles J. Halperin, "Russia in the Mongol Empire in Comparative Perspective," in the *Harvard Journal of Asiatic Studies* 43:1 (June, 1983).

Idem, Russia and the Golden Horde (Bloomington, 1985).

Janet Martin, "The Land of Darkness and the Golden Horde: The Fur Trade under the Mongols, XIII-XIV Centuries," in *Cahiers du Monde russe et sovietique* 19 (1978).

Nicholas V. Riasanovsky, "The Emergence of Eurasianism," in *California Slavic Studies* 4 (1967).

Valentin A. Riasanovsky, "The Influence of Ancient Mongol Culture and Law on Russian Culture and Law," in the *Chinese Social and Political Science Review* 20:4 (January, 1937).

Questions to Consider

1. How did the Tatars conquer Russia?
2. What kind of impact did the Golden Horde have on subsequent political and economic developments in Russia?
3. What was the nature of Tatar rule in Russia?

PART THREE

Russian History in the Muscovite Period

Chapter Eight

THE RISE OF MUSCOVY

During the reign of Ivan I (1325–41), called Kalita, or "Money-bags," the status of Moscow was substantially enhanced when, in 1328, he received the yarlyk from the Tatars. The yarlyk was the privilege-granting edict which gave the prince of Moscow, who was now called the Grand Prince (Velikii kniaz), the right to collect taxes from the Russian cities for the Golden Horde. It was not uncommon for the grand prince to request that the Tatars punish Moscow's commercial or political rivals on the pretext of non-payment of tribute. Further enhancing the status of the city was the arrival of the Metropolitan, who made Moscow his seat, thus making Moscow the religious center of all Russia.

Ironically, Moscow came to depict itself as a center of anti-Tatar agitation in the fourteenth century, and Muscovite propaganda exaggerated the significance of the victory of its grand prince Dmitri Donskoi (1359–89) over a Tatar army in the battle of Kulikovo (1380). More devastating for the Tatars than their loss at Kulikovo was their defeat by Timurlane in 1395, which resulted in the fragmentation of the Golden Horde into two smaller khanates centered on the Crimean peninsula and the Caspian Sea. For a full century following Kulikovo, however, the Russians continued to pay tribute to the Tatars. Payment finally ceased in 1480 during the reign of Ivan III "the Great" (1462–1505), when Moscow had acquired new prestige as the heir of Byzantine imperial tradition following the Ottoman Turkish conquest of Constantinople in 1453. Ivan married Zöe Paleologina (the niece of the last Byzantine emperor), who fled north to Russia with many Byzantine clerics and "bookmen" because it was the last bastion of Eastern Orthodoxy. These clerics and "bookmen" began to promote the "Doctrine of the Third Rome," in which Moscow was depicted as the direct political and spiritual heir of Rome and Constantinople. In line with this thinking, Ivan called himself Tsar' (Russian for Caesar).

Our first passage in this section consists of excerpts from The Nikonian Chronicle *concerning events during the reigns of Vasilii II (1425–62) and Ivan III (1462–1505). Produced under the supervision of the metropolitan of the Russian church, Daniil, in the 1520s,* The Nikonian Chronicle *contains important information on the Muscovite grand princes before Ivan IV. The text is translated by Serge A. Zenkovsky and Betty Jean Zenkovsky from the oldest version of the chronicle (the Obolenskii manuscript) published in St. Petersburg, 1854–1913. The second passage in this section is an excerpt from an epistle sent by brother Filofei of the Lazarus Monastery of Pskov to Grand Prince Vasilii III (1505–33), in which the "Doctrine of the Third Rome" is put forth (translated by Benson Bobrick).*

✢ The Epistle of Isidore, Metropolitan of Russia, Concerning the Union of the Roman Catholic and Greek Orthodox Churches (Resulting from the Council of Ferrara/Florence, 1439).[1]

"I, Isidore, by the grace of God Most Venerable Metropolitan of Kiev and all Russia, legate from the rib of the Apostle [*legatus latere*] for Poland, Lithuania and the Germans. Peace and blessing to all and to every faithful and true Christian who believes in eternal salvation from the Lord Jesus Christ. Rejoice and be of good cheer, all of you, concerning God because the Eastern church and the Roman church, which long were divided and were hostile one toward the other, now have become united in true unity according to their original union and peace, and there is quietude and love and the ancient single authority without any division. You all, people of Christ, whether you be Latin or Italian, or whether you be under the Holy Conciliar Greek Church of Constantinople to which the Russians, Serbs, Walachs and all other Christians belong who truly believe in Jesus Christ, Son of God, and God, Who created all—heaven and earth—and in Whom is all our life and all our hopes, now and ever, accept this holy and most sacred Union and single authority with great spiritual joy and honor.

"I beseech you all for the sake of Our Lord Jesus Christ, Who provided us with His grace, that there should not be any division between the Latins and you because everyone is the servant of God and Our Saviour Jesus Christ, and is baptized in His Name. There is One God, One Father, one baptism and there should be among you common agreement and tranquility and peace and love because of Jesus Christ. And you, people of the Latin faith, you should accept without any hesitation all those who are of the Greek faith. They all are baptized and their baptism is holy and recognized by the Roman church because it is true and it is the same as the one of the Roman church and one of the Eastern church. Beginning with now, there is not among us any mean mind or dissension in these matters. Both the Latins

---

1. Reprinted by permission of the publishers from Serge A. Zenkovsky (ed. and trans.) and Betty Jean Zenkovsky (co-trans.), *The Nikonian Chronicle* (Princeton, The Darwin Press, 1989), v. 5, pp. 58–59. This passage is excerpted from the entry *sub anno* 1441

Photo: The Belltowers of Ivan the Great, Moscow Kremlin.

and the aforementioned Greeks should go to the same unified church with a pure and humble heart, and they should bring their prayer and their supplication to be united in one unity unto the Lord God. And when the Greeks are in the Latin land and in case there are [only] Latin and Roman churches in some parts of these lands, they should go thither to the divine service with daring but humble heart and accept the Body of Christ with humble heart, and render honor there as they do in their own churches in their lands in which they live; and [in such cases] they have to come for confession to the Latin priests and accept from them the Body of Lord Jesus Christ, Our God. The Latins, likewise, have to go to the Greek churches and participate in their divine services with a warm faith and with humble heart, and venerate the same Body of Christ, because the One consecrated by the Greek priest in leavened bread is truly and wholly the Body of Christ as is That One Which is consecrated by the Latin priest in unleavened bread. And therefore we have to venerate both the leavened and the unleavened. And the Latins have to come for confession to the Greek priests and accept from them the holy and divine Communion because both are the same and true. And so it was decided by the great Oecumenic Council in their final meeting after many consultations and investigations of holy, divine writings in the honorable and great church in which was celebrated the church service and which is in the city of Florence. And it was on the sixth day of the month of June in the year 1439 after the Incarnation of Our Lord.''

✤ *How Metropolitan Isidore Escaped from Moscow to Rome*[1]

In the Year 6951 [1443]. On the fifteenth day of the month of September Metropolitan Isidore was enveloped by the darkness of his faithlessness and did not want to reject or repent the Union and agreement with the Latins. And he could not abide staying [under arrest] and waiting in the Monastery of the Miracles in Moscow and therefore, being faithless, he escaped secretly at night and fled with his pupils, Monks, Gregory and Athanasius. And from Moscow he went to Tver', from Tver' to Lithuania, and from thence to Rome to his Pope because he was conducted and instructed in his perdition by the devil. Grand Prince Vasilii Vasilievich, who was wise in God and greatly intelligent, did not send anyone to force him to return and did not want to keep him as a vain madman disgusting to God, and he did not want

---

1. Reprinted by permission of the publishers from Serge A. Zenkovsky (ed. and trans.) and Betty Jean Zenkovsky (co-trans.), *The Nikonian Chronicle* (Princeton, The Darwin Press, 1989), v. 5, pp. 66–67.

to be connected with the latter's sins, and did him no harm. And so Isidore went to Rome to Pope Eugenius, and from that time far away he continued to deal like an evil and destructive viper-devil, cruelly persecuting the Holy Church, which was blossoming in piety in the Russian dominion, and he [continued] to turn Christians to the Latin Faith and to Union and compromise. And Lord God and the Purest Mother of God protected the Holy Church of Russia from such an enemy smart in evil, and it will remain without blemish and discord. This occurred thanks to the great sovereign, Vasilii Vasilievich, who was a man of great sense and who was instructed by God. This most wise Tsar of all Russia greatly blossomed in piety; Lord God very wisely showed him how to understand everything, how to reckon and how to do the will of God, and how to preserve all His covenants.

✣ *The Burning of Moscow*[1]

On Wednesday, the fourteenth day of the same month of July, a fire started in the inner city of Moscow. This happened at night, and everything burned so that not a piece of wood remained in the city. The stone churches collapsed and even the stone walls of the fortifications collapsed in many places. A great many people burned: the monk-priests and priests, monks and nuns, and men, women, and children because this fire issued from thence [from the inner city], and they were afraid to go outside the walls because they feared the Tatars. And great wealth and an endless amount of all sorts of goods burned because a great number of people from many cities had taken refuge in Moscow. When the city burned, the Grand Princess Sofia and Grand Princess Maria with their children and boyars went to the city of Rostov, and the citizens were in great despond and became agitated. Those who could sought to leave the city. The common people assembled, however, and began to restore the city gates and started catching and thrashing those who wanted to escape from thence, and even put [some] in irons. And so the panic came to an end and everyone together set to fortifying the city and building houses for themselves.

---

1. Reprinted by permission of the publishers from Serge A. Zenkovsky (ed. and trans.) and Betty Jean Zenkovsky (co-trans.), *The Nikonian Chronicle* (Princeton, the Darwin Press, 1989), v. 5, p. 75. This excerpt is taken from the entry *sub anno* 1445.

❖ *The Earthquake of 1446*[1]

On the first of October of the same fall, the very day the Grand Prince was released from Kurmish, at six o'clock at night, the earth shook in the city of Moscow, in the Kremlin, in the suburbs, and all the churches shook. Many people who were asleep at the time did not hear it at all. Others, who were not sleeping, heard it and were greatly distressed, afraid for their lives, and in the morning they told of it tearfully to those who had not heard. The same fall during St. Philip's Fast the Grand Prince confessed and had Communion, and came to Moscow on the seventeenth day of November, staying at the court of his mother in Vagankovo, outside the city. Thereafter he journeyed into the city to the mansion of Prince Iurii Patrikeevich.

---

1. Reprinted by permission of the publishers from Serge A. Zenkovsky (ed. and trans.) and Betty Jean Zenkovsky (co-trans.), *The Nikonian Chronicle* (Princeton, The Darwin Press, 1989), v. 5, p. 77.

❖ *The Natural Disasters*[1]

On the thirty-first of the month of August at the first hour of the night there was frightful thunder and great lightning, as if it wanted to set a fire. But there was a heavy downpour. This lightning destroyed the top of the stone church in the Simeon Monastery, up to the windows. And moving around the church, it hit the arch and then it broke through the wall at the front entrance and destroyed many holy icons. The icon of the Dormition and the icon of the Prophets were destroyed, and the icon of *Deisus* was singed by the lightning. And the icon of the Most Pure *Hadigitria,* which stands protected on the left side, was not touched, although stone fell around at the *grivnas* which were attached to it.

In the year 6985 [1477]. On the third of the month of September, at night, the full moon disappeared during August.

The sixth of the same month the Grand Prince let the Tatar envoy, Bochiuk, go, and with him went his envoy, Matvei Bestuzhev.

---

1. Reprinted by permission of the publishers from Serge A. Zenkovsky (ed. and trans.) and Betty Jean Zenkovsky (co-trans.), *The Nikonian Chronicle* (Princeton, The Darwin Press, 1989), p. 176. These excerpts are taken from entries *sub annis* 1476–77.

The twenty-sixth of the same month the Church of the Ascension on the Moat in Moscow burned.

✤ *The Doctrine of the Third Rome*[1]

One ruler of the present orthodox Empire is on earth the sole Emperor of the Christians, the leader of the Apostolic Church which stands no longer in Rome or in Constantinople, but in the blessed city of Moscow. She alone shines in the whole world brighter than the sun. . . . All Christian Empires are fallen and in their stead stands alone the Empire of our ruler in accordance with the prophetical books. Two Romes have fallen, but the third stands and a fourth there will not be.

---

1. Reproduced from Benson Bobrick, *Fearful Majesty: The Life and Reign of Ivan the Terrible* (New York, Putnam, 1987), p. 76

Chapter Nine

THE REIGN OF IVAN IV GROZNY

*The reign of Ivan IV Grozny ("the Terrible"
or "the Dread;" 1533–84) marked a turning
point in Russian history. Ivan assumed the title
of Tsar' at his coronation and many historians
have emphasized the autocratic nature of the*
tsardom. *He created a uniformed, paramilitary service nobility, called the
Oprichnikii, who operated as the tsar's agents within the one-third of Russia
set aside for them, the Oprichnina. Many of the boyars' estates were confis-
cated within the Oprichnina, where peasants as well as the old aristocracy
lost rights and privileges and were subject to the arbitrary rule of the Oprichnikii. The boyars, however, retained their traditional rights within the
rest of Russia, the Zemshchina (Russian "land"). Ivan also created a corps
of musketeers, the Streltsi, whose importance superceded that of the mounted
warrior aristocracy whose service to the grand princes was traditionally
based on land grants (pomesties).*

*Ivan conquered some of the Tatar khanates that had emerged after the
defeat of the Golden Horde by Timurlane, Kazan (1552) and Astrakhan
(1554), as well as the Khanate of Sibir (1581) under the Stroganovs and
Cossacks led by Yermak. The conquest of the Khanate of Sibir, in Siberia,
aided Moscow economically by bringing in large tracts of agricultural land
and many forests which contained fur-bearing animals. Many Russian furs
and other products of the forest were traded in this period to England. A
sign of the importance of Russia's commercial contacts with England is observed in the large volume of extant correspondence between the English
and Muscovite courts, and in the marriage proposal made by Ivan to Elizabeth (but turned down by the "Virgin Queen").*

*Following the end of the Tatar Yoke, Russian rulers tried to expand their
diplomatic and commercial ties with Western Europe. In the course of this
"outreach", special missions and embassies were sent to England, and the
Muscovy Company was established to facilitate and control Russian-English
trade.*

*The English public, in turn, was curious about the Russians, whom they
also called Muscovites or Muscovits, but tended to adopt a deprecating attitude towards them, an attitude which is expressed, for example, by Rosaline,
a major character in William Shakespeare's comedy Love's Labor's Lost.
Although Rosaline's remarks pertain to three English gentlemen, whose dis-*

*guise as Russian emissaries has been penetrated, the opinions expressed
were clearly meant to apply equally well to the real Russian envoys visiting
Elizabethan England:*

> *Rosaline.* Good madam, if by me you'll be advised,
> Let's mock them still as well known as disguised:
> Let us complain to them what fools were here.
> Disguised like Muscovites, in shapeless gear;
> And wonder what they were, and to what end
> Their shallow shows and prologue vilely penned,
> And their rough carriage so ridiculous,
> Should be presented at our tent to us.

*Fur was a Russian export to England, and it is not surprising that the
biggest and fiercest of Russia's fur-bearing animals, the bear, should attract
special attention. And so did the cold Russian climate. Thus, Shakespeare,
who was superbly sensitive to the opinions, beliefs, and usages of his countrymen, refers to the "rugged Russian bear" in* Macbeth, *and suggests in*
Henry V *that the "mouth of the Russian bear" was no place to be; while in*
Love's Labor's Lost, *Russians are described as "frozen muscovits."*

Russians are mentioned twice in Shakespeare's Measure for Measure, *and
in his* Winter's Tale, *Hermione asserts outright that the "Emperor of Russia" was her father. The misapprehension that Russia was ruled by Emperors was apparently common enough in Elizabethan England, for it also
occurs in other sources of the period. In reality, however, Russian rulers did
not adopt the Imperial title until 1721.*

Our first passage in this section is from the History of the Grand Duke of
Muscovy, *completed circa 1573 by Prince Andrei Mikhailovich Kurbsky.
Kurbsky served on Ivan's Boyar Council and was a military leader in Ivan's
wars against the Livonians and the Lithuanians. He fell out of favor with the
tsar', however, in 1563 and soon fled to Lithuania, from which location he
wrote a series of letters to Ivan, criticizing the suppression of the nobility.
Kurbsky wrote his* History *as a polemical work to demonstrate the flaws in
Ivan's character and the injustices he committed against the nobility. The
work nevertheless contains much useful information about Ivan and six-
teenth-century Muscovy. The text is translated by J. L. I. Fennell from a
1914 edition produced by the Imperial Archaeological Commission, which
utilized four late-seventeenth-century manuscripts.*

The second passage, from The History of the Most Renowned and Victo-
rious Princess Elizabeth, Late Queen of England, *by William Camden, de-
scribes the commercial relationship between England and Russia from the
English perspective. Master and then Headmaster of the Westminster School,
Camden was urged to write his history by Elizabeth's treasurer, Lord
Burghley. The work, which utilized official royal documents, was completed*

in 1617 and was published in Latin and English versions. The version used here is the English translation of 1688, edited by Wallace T. MacCaffrey.

The third passage consists of official correspondence between Ivan and Elizabeth, collected and edited by George Tolstoy. Many Englishmen visited Russia during Ivan's reign, negotiating commercial deals and recording what they observed in diaries. One of these visitors was Robert Best, who served as an interpreter. Best published The Voyage wherein Osepp Napea, the Moscovite Ambassador, Returned Home into his Country *in 1557, and it is from this text that our fourth passage, "The Blessing of the Waters," is taken. The final passage in this section is an anonymous contemporary* bylina *(heroic oral song) describing Ivan's corpse as it lay in state, translated by W. R. Morfill.*

✥ *Kurbsky's History of Ivan IV*[1]

But as for what he used to do when he came of age, at about twelve or later, I will be silent on most things; however this I will relate. At first he began to spill the blood of dumb creatures, hurling them from lofty places (in their language: from porches or from the top stories of houses) and to do many other unbefitting things as well, betraying in himself the future merciless will; for, as Solomon says: "a wise man regardeth the life of his beasts; likewise the foolish man beats them unsparingly". But while his tutors flattered him by allowing this and praising him, they taught the child to their own detriment. And when he came to his fifteenth year, he began to harm people. Gathering around him groups of youths and relatives of those above-mentioned counsellors, he rode with them on horseback through the squares and market-places and beat and robbed the common people, men and women, indecorously galloping and racing everywhere. And in truth he committed real acts of brigandage and performed other evil deeds which it is not only unbefitting to relate, but shameful too; and all his flatterers would praise such behaviour, to their own detriment, saying: "O, brave and manly will this tsar be!" But when he came to his seventeenth year, then those same arrogant counsellors began to urge him on and through him to avenge their hostilities, one against the other. And first of all they killed a most powerful man, a very brave general and a man of great stock, who came from the kin of the princes of Lithuania, of the same family as King Jagiello of Poland, Prince Ivan Bel'sky by name, who was not only manly, but was great in intellect and versed in the holy scriptures.

And after a short time he himself ordered a certain noble prince by the name of Andrey Shuysky, from the kin of the princes of Suzdal', to be put to death. Then, after about two years, he killed three men of great stock: one, a near kinsman, born of the sister of his father, Prince Ioann Kubensky, who had been the great marshal of the land at his father's court; and he was of the kin of the princes of Smolensk and Yaroslavl' and a man of great wisdom and gentleness, already of mature years; and together with him were killed the above-mentioned [sic] men, Fedor and Vasily Vorontsov, born of German stock from the kin of the imperial princes. And then Fedor Nevezha was killed, a distinguished and rich landowner. And shortly before this,

1. Reprinted by permission of the publishers from J. L. I. Fennell (ed. and trans.), *Prince A.M. Kurbsky's History of Ivan IV* (Cambridge, U.K. and New York, Cambridge University Press, 1965), pp. 11, 13, 15, 17, 25, 51, 57.

Photo: St. Basil's Cathedral in Moscow, built by Ivan IV Grozny to commemorate his victories over the Tatars.

about two years earlier, the son of Prince Bogdan Trubetskoy was executed by him, an infant of fifteen years, Mikhail by name, from the kin of the princes of Lithuania. And then, I recall, in the same year the following noble princes were killed by him: Prince Ioann Dorogobuzhsky, from the kin of the grand princes of Tver', and Fedor Ovchina, the only son of Prince Ioann, from the kin of the princes of Torusa and Obolensk, slaughtered in their innocence like lambs, with the first down of manhood still on their cheeks. After that, when he began to surpass himself in all kinds of countless evil deeds, the Lord tempered his ferocity by visiting the great city of Moscow with an exceedingly large fire and thus manifestly inflicted His wrath—if one were to write about it all in turn, there could be a whole story or a small book; but before this, while he was still in his youth, [God visited the land] with countless barbarian conquests, now by the khan [lit. "tsar"] of Pere-kop, now by the Nogay Tartars, that is to say those from beyond the Volga; but more and worse than all, by the khan of Kazan', the strong and powerful tormenter of Christians, who in his power held six different tribes, by means of which he brought about countless and ineffable conquests and bloodshed so that everything was barren for eighteen miles before the town of Moscow; and also the whole land of Ryazan', right up to the very Oka river, was laid waste by the khan of Perekop, or Crimea, and by the Nogays; while within the country the men-pleasers, together with the young tsar, laid waste and mercilessly ravaged the fatherland. And then occurred, after that above-mentioned exceedingly large and in truth most terrible fire, in which no one will hesitate to discern the manifest wrath of God—but what occurred then?

There was a great tumult of all the people, so that the tsar himself had to run away from the town with his court; and in that tumult his uncle Prince Yury Glinsky was killed by the common people and all his house was plundered; and his other uncle Prince Mikhail Glinsky, who was the author of all evil, ran away, and other men-pleasers who were with him dispersed. And at that time in a somewhat wondrous way God stretched out the hand of help, [allowing] the Christian land to rest, in this manner: at that time, I say, there came to him a man, a priest by rank, by name Sil'vestr, a newcomer from Novgorod the Great, divinely rebuking him with holy scriptures and sternly conjuring him in the terrible name of God; and furthermore telling him of miracles and apparitions sent as it were by God. (I do not know if they were true or if he devised them for himself in order to scare him because of his folly and his childish unbridled ways; just as fathers often order their servants to scare their children with imaginary horrors and [to turn them] from the senseless games of their wicked playfellows, so too did this blessed man, I think, add to his well-meaning cunning a little threat, with which he planned to heal a great evil). For physicians do this in case of need, scraping and cutting the putrid gangrene with a knife, or cutting away the raw flesh which grows on the wound even as far as the live flesh. And perhaps in a similar way to this did that blessed man, the true deceiver, plan; for so it followed: he healed and purified his soul from leprous sores and rectified his depraved mind, in this way guiding him to the right path.

And straightway, with the help of God, the Christian army prevailed against the enemies. And against which enemies? The great and awesome Ishmaelite race, before which the whole universe once trembled—and not only did the universe tremble, but it was even laid waste by them. And not against one khan only did they take up arms but straightway against three great and powerful khans—to wit against the khan of Perekop, against the khan of Kazan' and against the Nogay princes. And with the grace and help of Christ our God from that time forward they drove off invasion by all three, won frequent conquests and bedecked themselves with most glorious victories; indeed were I to relate all of them in turn, this short tale would not suffice to contain them. To put it briefly: during a few years the boundaries of our Christian land were expanded not only to the extent of the devastation which the Russian land had suffered from them, but to a far greater degree; for where previously, in the devastated Russian districts, there had been Tatar winter-quarters, there fortresses and towns were built. And not only did the horses of the sons of Russia drink from the flowing rivers in Asia, from the Tanais and the Kuala and others, but even fortresses were built there.

And in about two days they came to the town of Arsk which I have mentioned and they found it empty and abandoned, for all had fled in fear from it into the most distant forests. And they ravaged the land for about ten days, for in that land there are great plains, which are most fertile and which abound in all kinds of fruits; also the courts of their princes and magnates are extremely fine and indeed amazing, and the villages are frequent. As for grain, there are so many different kinds that it would indeed be hard to believe, were one to tell of them all—it would be like the multitude of the stars in the sky. There are, too, countless herds of different kinds of cattle and there is valuable profit to be had especially from the various wild beasts which are in that land; for costly martens breed there and squirrels and other animals which can be used for clothing and for food. Furthermore there are a great number of sables and also many kinds of honey—I know not where beneath the sun there are more. And after ten days they returned safely to us with incalculable booty and with a multitude of captive Mussulman wives and children; and also they freed from long-lasting slavery many of their countrymen, who had long ago been captured by the Mussulmans. And at that time there was great rejoicing in the Christian army and we sang our thanks to God, and in our army all forms of livestock were cheaper—one could buy a cow for ten Moscow *den'gi* and a large ox for ten squirrel skins.

But we, according to the orders given to us, prepared for the attack early—about two hours before dawn: I had been sent to assault the lower gates from upstream on the Kazan' river, and I had with me twelve thousand troops. On all four sides mighty and valiant men were drawn up, some of them with large detachments. When the khan of Kazan' and his counsellors learned about this, they too prepared against us as we had against them.

Just before the rising of the sun, or a little after it had begun to appear, the underground passage exploded and the Christian army immediately attacked the town and the fortress on all sides, according to the order of the tsar. Let each man tell of his own deeds; I will briefly and truthfully narrate what I had before my own eyes at that time and what I did. I allocated my twelve thousand troops to their various commanders and we ran up to the walls of the fortress, to that great tower which stood on a hill in front of the gates. When we were still quite far off from the walls, we were not fired at from a single musket or bow; but when we got near, then for the first time fire was directed on us from the walls and from the towers. The arrows fell so thickly that they were like heavy rain, and so incalculably great was the number of stones that the sky could not be seen! And when we had fought our way up to the wall with great difficulty and suffering, they began to pour boiling water on us and to hurl whole beams at us. None the less God helped us by giving us bravery and strength and forgetfulness of death, and in truth with cheerful heart and with joy we fought the Mussulmans for Orthodox Christianity; and within about half an hour we drove them away from the embrasures with arrows and musket fire. Furthermore, the guns from behind our trenches helped us, firing at them; for they now stood openly at that great tower and on the walls of the fortress, not concealing themselves as before, but fighting fiercely with us, face to face and hand to hand. And we might straightway have killed them all, but, although many of us took part in the assault, few came right up to the walls of the fortress: some went back and many lay on the ground pretending to be killed or wounded.

❖ *William Camden's Account of Russian-English Commercial Contacts*[1]

About this time came into England Stephen Twerdico and Theodore Pogorella, from the most potent Emperour John Basilides, Emperour of Russia and Moscovia, with rich Furs of Sables, Luserns, and others, which at that time and in former Ages were in great request amongst the English, both for their Ornament and Wholesomeness. They made large Offers of all Kindness and Assistence to the Queen and the English, which the said Emperour had already abundantly shewed upon these beginnings following.

Whilst certain Merchants of London, whereof the chief were Andrew Judd, George Barns, William Gerard, and Anthony Husey, in the year 1553 fought a way into Cathay by the Frozen or North Sea, under the Conduct of Sir Huge Willoughby, who was frozen to death, Richard Chanceller next after him happily discovered a Passage into Russia, which was before unknown, being brought into the mouth of the River Dwina, under the 64th degree of Latitude of the North Pole, where standeth a little Monastery dedicated to Saint Nicholas. From hence the Emperour sent for them to Mosco by Sleds drawn over the Ice, after the manner of the Courtney: he welcomed them kindly, and dismissed them bountifully, promising large Privileges to the English, if they would traffick in his Empire; heartily rejoycing that Outlandish Merchandizes might be brought into Russia by Sea, which the Russians had before with difficulty received by Narva and the hostile Countries of the Polonian. When Chanceller was returned, and reported these things, and how dear the English Cloaths were sold in those parts, and how cheap Hemp and Flax for Cables, Wax and rich Furrs were sold unto them; those Merchants grew into a Company or Society, by the Assent of Queen Mary, which we call the Moscovia Company, who, having many Privileges granted them by Basilides, from that time had a rich Trade of it, sending every year a Fleet thither. But most gainfull it was to them after that, through Queen Elizabeth's Favour with Basilides, they obtained in the year 1569 that none but the English Merchants of that Company should trade in the North parts of Russia, and that they alone should vend their Merchandizes all over that most spacious Empire, as in proper place we will declare.

---

1. Reprinted by permission of the publishers from William Camden, *The History of the Most Renowned and Victorious Princess Elizabeth, Late Queen of England,* ed. by Wallace T. McCaffrey (Chicago, University of Chicago Press, 1970), pp. 79–80; 107–09; 158–60.

With these Russian Embassadours returned into England Anthony Jenkinson, who took a most exact Survey of Russia, described it in a Geographical Map, and was the first Englishman that sailed on the Caspian Sea, and made his way to the Bactrians. To this Jenkinson the Emperour gave certain secret Instructions, which he imparted not to his own people: to wit, "That he should seriously solicite the Queen for a mutual League of Defense and Offence against all men, and to send Ship wrights, Sailers and Munition into Russia: and that the Queen would bind her self by Oath to receive him courteously with his Wife and Children, if he should be thrown out of his Kingdom either by Rebels or Enemies." Thus did a Tyrant, from whom no man can keep any thing safe, seem to himself to be without Safety. And certainly he took it ill that the Queen answered slightly to these Points. And yet he ceased not both by Letters and Embassie to urge these things, as in due place we will shew, now and then requiring that the said Anthony might be sent back, as if he had dealt unfaithfully in Secrets of so great a moment.

In these days the Traffick of the English Merchants was no less obstructed in Russia than in the Netherlands, as well by means of the false Dealing of their Factours, and their untoward Dissension amongst themselves, as of the Germans and Russians Hatred against them: whilst the Russians complained of their cunning Dealing, and the raising of the Prices to their Merchandizes: and the English which were not of the Muscovia Company and Germans complained of the Monopoly. To salve those Soars, Thomas Randolph was sent the last year into Russia: who though he were not very welcome to the Emperour, forasmuch, as he seriously solicited onely the matter of Trade, and mentioned nothing at all of the League which I have spoken of before in the year 1567; nevertheless at his Intercession the Emperour, out of his singular Good will to the Queen and the English Nation, granted to the English Company in Russia Freedom from all payment of Custome, and Liberty to carry and vend their Merchandizes wheresoever they would throughout all the Countries of his most spatious Empire, and to transport them into Persia and Media by the Caspian Sea (whereas the Merchants of other Nations might not go a mile beyond the City of Moskow;) he gave them also Houses to twist their Ropes and Cables into for Shipping, and a piece of Ground five miles in circuit with Wood to make Iron, and took the English into an *Opprisney,* that is, into a choice Seed of his people.

And now the English began more confidently to survey those Countries, carrying their Merchandizes up the River Dwina in Boats made of one whole Piece or Tree, which they rowed and towed up the Stream with Halsers, as far as Wologda; and from thence by land seven days journey to Yeraslaw; and then, by the Wolga, (which is about a mile over, and runneth through a clayish Soil, beset with Oaks and Birchen-trees,), thirty days and as many nights Journey down the River to Astracan. And from Astracan (where they built Ships) they did (which was a very great and memorable Adventure) many times cross the Caspian Sea, which is very full of Flats and Shelves, and pierced through the vast Desarts of Hyrcania and Bactriana to Teverin and Casbin, Cities of Persia, in hope at length to discover Cathay. But the Wars which shortly after grew hot between the Turks and Persians, and the Robberies of the Barbarians, interrupted this laudable Enterprise of the Londoners. The Emperour sent back Randolph with Presents, and with him Andreas Gregoriwitz Saviena, with a splendid Train, after the manner of the Nation, who was gallantly entertained by the Londoners, and honourably received by the Queen. This Andreas shewed a certain League written in the Russian Tongue, which he required might be ratified by secret Letters in the self-same words in his presence, and be translated with all the Letters into the Russian Tongue, and confirmed by the Queen's Hand, Seal and Oath: as also that the Queen would send an Embassadour of her own into Russia, who in like manner should receive secret Letters of the Emperour's in the same words, confirmed with his Seal and the kissing of the Cross in his presence. The Queen concluded the League with a Clause of Reservation, "So far forth as she lawfully might by the League formerly contracted with other Princes, to yield one another mutual Aid against their common Enemies, so as nothing should be done against Law and Right." And if he should by any Misfortune be constrained, either by domestical or foreign Enemies, to leave his Countrey, she promised most religiously in the word of a Christian Princess, before his Embassadour and her inwardest Counsellours, and confirmed it with her Seal, to receive and entertain him, his Wife and Children, with all Honour worthy so great a Prince, to assign him a convenient place for his Abode, to permit him the free Exercise of his Religion, and Liberty to depart at his pleasure: for these were the things which he had earnestly intreated in those secret Letters. But so far was all this from satisfying that fierce-natur'd man, to whom his own mind and will was a Law, that in a long Letter having reckoned all his Civilities to the English Nation, he twittingly upbraided them therewith, stomached that the Queen sent not an Embassadour with his to receive his Oath, and taxed her as if she neglected him, and were too mindfull of the Merchants Business, (which were matters unbeseeming a Prince;) which Merchants he contemptuously and disgracefully charged as a sordid kind of people, that rather gaped after Wealth than fought their Prince's honour, suspecting that they crossed his Designs, and sharply threatening to recall their Privileges. Which notwithstanding he did not, being pacified by a kind Letter of the Queen's sent by Jenkinson, but most diligently observed her as his Sister as long as he lived, solicited her many times for a more solid Confirmation of the said League, and loved the English passing well above all other nations.

It is not here to be forgot how in these days, War growing hot betwixt the Moscovite and the Swede in the Northern Climate, John King of Sweden, unable to resist the Power of so great an Emperour, sent Eric of Wisimbrug, his Kinsman, Andreas Riche one of his Council, and Raschy his Secretary, on a noble Embassy to Q. Elizabeth, and by his Letters intreated her to mediate Peace with the Moscovite by her Embassadour: which she did without Delay, and perswaded the Moscovite to a Peace upon reasonable Conditions. For he dealt now afresh with the Queen about the League before-mentioned, and about his Refuge in England if any Disaster should befall him; and made Suit also for a Wife out of England. Touching these matters Sir Hierome Bowes Knight was sent Embassadour thither, but could hardly satisfie him, for that the Moscovite with much Importunity required an absolute League written in his own words; and would by no means hear that it was not the part of a Christian, nor allowable by the Law of Nations, to exercise Hostility without first denouncing War, or to come to Blows before such time as he that offered the Wrong were required to give Satisfaction, and to abstain from doing further Injury. The Queen designed him for a Wife the Lady Anne, Sister to the Earl of Huntingdon. But when she certainly understood that he might, by the Laws of his Countrey, put away his Wives at his pleasure; she excused it again by the Lady's Imposition of Health, and the tender Affection of her Mother, who could not endure the Absence of her Daughter in a Countrey so far distant, and that she had no power to give the Daughters of her Subjects in Marriage without the Consent of their Parents. Nevertheless the Embassadour prevailed with him to conform the Merchants Privileges: but his Death ensuing the year following, the Trade of the English in Russia, withall decayed by little and little, and the Embassadour was sent back, who returned not without Danger of his Life, and was received by the Queen with Favour and Commendations. He was the first (if an Historian may have leave to mention so trivial a matter) who brought into England the Beast called a *Machlis,* never before seen here: it is like the Beast called an Elk, in Latine *Alce,* but having no Joynts in the Legs, and yet wonderfull swift. He brought also certain Fallow-deer of admirable Swiftness, which being yoked together would draw a man sitting in a Sled with incredible Speed.

Theodore Joannides, the Son of John Basilides, (to joyn Moscovia matters together) succeeded in that vast Empire; a Prince of a duller Spirit, but yet one that would hearken to them that gave him good Counsel. This Theodore granted to all Merchants of what Nation soever free Access into Russia: and being oftentimes solicited by the Queen to confirm the Privileges granted by his Father to the Moscovia Company of English Merchants, to wit, that onely English-men of that Company should come into or trade in the North parts of Russia, and that Custome-free, in regard they were the first that discovered the Passage thither by Sea; he thereupon desired her to give Liberty to all the English to trade into Russia: for to permit some, and deny others, was Injustice. Princes, he said, must carry an indifferent land betwixt their Subjects, and not convert Trade (which by the Law of Nations ought to be common to all) into a Monopoly to the private Gain of a few. As for his Customs, he promised to exact less by the one half of that Company than of the rest, because they first discovered the Passage thither by Sea. In other matters he confirmed their former Privileges, and added some few more out of his Respect to the Queen, and not for any Desert (as he said) of the Company, many of whom he found had dealt falsely with his People. And other Answer than this could Giles Fletcher, Doctour of Law, who was afterwards sent Embassadour on the same Account, get none. This Fletcher set forth a little Book of the Russian Polity or Tyranny, wherein are many things worthy of Observation. Which Book notwithstanding was quickly suppressed, lest it might give Offense to a Prince in Amity with England.

✣ *Official Correspondence Between Elizabeth and Ivan*[1]

No. 12—1567 Nov.

Antho. Jenkinsons message done to the Q. Ma-tie from the Emperor of Moscouia.

Ffirst, the said Emperor of Muscouia earnestly requireth that there may be a perpetuall frendship and kyndred betwixt the Q. ma-tie and him which shalbe the begining of further matter to be done.

Ffurther the said Emperour requireth that the Q. ma-tie and he might be (to all their enemyes) joyned as one; to say her grace to be ffreind to his friends and enemy to his enemyes, and so per contr. And that England and Russland might be in all matters, as one.

Ffurther the said prynce hath willed to declare to the Q. ma-tie that as the king of Pole' is not his ffreind, even so he sheweth himself not to be frend to the Q. ma-tie ffor that this last somer ther was a spye taken with lettres from the king of Pole' directed to the English merchants in Russia, wherin

1. Reprinted from George Tolstoy, ed. *The First Forty Years of Correspondence between England and Russia, 1553–1593* (New York, Burt Franklin, 1964), pp. 38–39; 90–91.

was written thiese wordes. I, Sigismond, K. of Pole' etc. require you Englysh marchants my trustie servants to aide this bringer, and to assist and ayde such Russes as be my ffreinds with money and all other helpes, with other wordes. Wherat the Emperor at the ffirst was much offended. But after by the confession of the spie (when he suffred death) it was knowne to be a practize of the k. of Pole', as well to haue by that meanes caused the indignacon of the Emperor to haue fallen upon the English nation and to haue broken ffrendship betwixt the Q. ma-tie and him, As allso that he should haue charged diuers of his nobles with treason Wherfore the Emperor requireth the Q. ma-tie that she would bee and joyne with him (as one) upon the Pole and not to suffer her people to haue trade of merchandize, with the subjects of the K. of Pole'.

Ffurther, the Emperor requireth that the Q's ma-tie would lycence maisters to come unto him which can make shippes, and sayle them.

Ffurther that the Q. ma-tie would suffer him to haue out of England all kynde of Artillerie and things necessarie for warre.

Ffurther the Emperor requireth earnestly that there may be assurance made by oath and faith betwixt the Q. ma-tie and him, that yf any misfortune might fall or chance upon ether of them to goe out of their countries, that it might be lawfull to ether of them to come into the others countrey for the safegard of them selues and their lyves, And ther to lyve and haue relief without any feare or danger untill such tyme as such misfortune be past, and that god hath otherwise provided, and that the one may be receaved of the other with honour. And this to be keapt most seacret.

And of all this matter, the Emperor requireth the Q. ma-tie most humbly to have answer by some of her trustie councellours, or by one of more greater estimacon then myself. And whatsoever the Q-s m -tie shall require of him, yt shall be granted and fully accomplished:

The Queenes ma-tie answere to be geven, the Emperour requyreth. by S-t Peters day next.

No. 25—1570 May 18.

Elizabeth to Ivan Basily.

Because we vnderstand from you Emperour and great Duke our good brother first by the report of our trustie servant Anthony Jenkinson whom we sent as our embassadour to you *the* emperor, certen yeres past, and now last by your embassadour the noble parson Andrew Gregoriwiche Saviena and with hym your secretary Sevastyana whom ye sent to vs as your highnes ambassadours in company with our last ambassadour Thomas Randolph, that you the said emperour do ernestly deseir to enteir into some streight contracts of amity with vs, and for that purpose where the said Andrew Gregoriwich hath delivered vnto vs certen writings in the Russian tongue, which becawse we could not vnderstand for lack of knowledg of that tongue, the said ambassadour hath deliverd to vs in certen other writings both in the Romane tongue and in the Italian, which are sayd to be the trew translations of the said lettres in the Russian tongue: both which (wrytyngs) we do well vnderstand and therby do conceave that the said writings are devised only as a forme of such a league and confederation, as you—our deare brother emperour—wold have with vs for a mutuall streight amity: whervpon we have with good deliberation resolved to accept in most friendly manner this the offer of the good will of so mighty a prince, and to contract amity with yow the said emperour, so farr furth as the treaties and confederations which we have had of long time and receaved by succession of our progenitors kings of England (and do yet continew) with ether Christian princes emperours kinges and potentats may *any wise* permitt vs. And in consideration of your the said mighty emperours favour shewd to our *loving* subjects trading your contreys for merchandize and *specially* in respect of your further—inward and secret—disposition which by sundry good meanes we are informed ye beare towards vs: we are pleased to contract with yow—emperour and great duke—as followeth with the same words as nere as we may, as we find conteyned in your highnes writings as *they ar translated.*

We enter into a frendly and sisterly league to continew for ever with yow—great Lord and Emperour—as a mighty prince and our deare brother Emperour Lord and great Duke of all Russia. Which league we will so observe and kepe forever, as to bind ourselves with our *mvtuall and* commen forces to *withstand and* offend all such as shalbe commen enemies to vs both and to defend both our princely honours the estate of our realmes and contreys and to help ayde and favour eache of vs the other with mutuall helpes and aydes against our commen enemies as farrfurth as the effect of these our lettres shall stretche.

✣ Robert Best: The Blessing of the Waters[1]

Every yeere, upon the twelfe day, they use to blesse or sanctifie the river *Moska,* which runneth through the citie of *Moskovia,* after this manner.

First, they make a square hole in the ice about 3 fadoms large every way, which is trimmed about the sides and edges with white boords. Then about 9. of the clocke they come out of the church with procession towards the river in this wise.

First and foremost, there goe certaine yong men with Waxe tapers burning, and one carying a great lanterne. Then follow certaine banners, then the crosse, then the images of our Ladie, of S. Nicholas, and of other Saints, which images men carrie upon their shoulders. After the images follow certaine priests, to the number of 100 or more; after them the Metropolitan, who is led betweene two priests; and after the Metropolitan came the Emperour, with his crowne upon his head; and after his maiestie all his noble men orderly. Thus they folowed the procession unto the water; & when they came unto the hole that was made, the priests set themselves in order round about it. And at one side of the same poole there was a scaffold of boords made, upon which stood a faire chaire, in which the Metropolitan was set, but the Emperours maiestie stood upon the ice.

After this the priests began to sing, to blesse and to sense, and did their service, and so by that time that they had done the water was holy, which being sanctified, the Metropolitane tooke a little thereof in his handes and cast it on the Emperour, likewise upon certaine of the Dukes, and then they returned againe to the church with the priests that sate about the water. But ye preasse [press] that there was about the water when the Emperor was gone was wonderful to behold, for there came about 5,000. pots to be filled of that water; for that Muscovite which hath no part of that water thinks himselfe unhappy.

And very many went naked into the water, both men and women and children. After the prease was a little gone, the Emperours Jennets and horses were brought to drink of the same water, and likewise many other men brought their horses thither to drinke; and by that means they make their horses as holy as themselves.

---

1. Reprinted with permission of Atheneum Publishers, an imprint of Macmillan Publishing Company, from *Moscow: A Travellers' Companion,* by Laurence Kelly, ed. Copyright © 1983 by Laurence Kelly.

✢ Ivan's Body Lying in State in the Uspensky Cathedral of Michael the Archangel[1]

There stood a new-made coffin of cypress wood;
In the coffin lies the Orthodox Tsar—
The Orthodox Tsar, Ivan Vasilievich, the Terrible;
The life-giving cross stands at its head;
By the cross lies the imperial crown;
At his feet the terrible sword;
Every one prays to the life-giving cross;
Every one bows to the golden diadem;
Every one looks with trembling at the terrible sword.

---

1. Reproduced from W. R. Morfill, *The Story of Russia* (New York, G. P. Putnam's Sons, 1890), p. 89.

Chapter Ten

THE TIME OF TROUBLES AND THE ACCESSION OF THE ROMANOVS

Following the death of Ivan IV in 1584, his son Feodor I succeeded him. Feodor's reign (1584–88) was dominated by his brother-in-law Boris Godunov, and ambitious and talented former oprichnik who had been a close associate of Ivan. As regent for Feodor, Boris presided over a separate court and was responsible for the elevation of the metropolitanate of the Russian church into an autocephalous patriarchate. The old Muscovite dynasty was fated to end when Feodor's younger brother Dmitri died in 1591, as Feodor and his wife were unable to bear children. Although many rival courtiers believed Boris to have been responsible for Dmitri's death, the specially-convened Zemski Sobor (national assembly) elected Boris Tsar' when Feodor died in 1598.

Boris ruled as Tsar' until 1605. His reign was plagued by drought, resulting in crop failures and famines, which in turn led to civil unrest. At the close of his reign, Russia was invaded by a Polish army whose purpose was ostensibly to restore Dmitri to his throne (this "False Dmitri," however, was actually a defrocked monk named Grigori Otrepiev). Boris died of natural causes in the midst of the Polish invasion and disaffected boyars killed his widow and son. The Poles captured Moscow, but were ejected later with the help of a volunteer popular army led by Minin (a butcher by trade) and Prince Pozharsky. Russia remained in a state of turmoil for eight years, which period is known as the Time of Troubles (1605–13). During the Time of Troubles, False Dmitri was removed from power, replaced by the powerful boyar Vasilii Shuiski (1606–10), who was himself removed by rivals who initiated a three-year time of political chaos in which boyar factions fought with and against the Polish King Sigismund, and two more False Dmitris emerged. In 1613, a Zemski Sobor ended the chaos by electing Mikhail Romanov as the new Tsar'. Mikhail's cause was strengthened by the fact that the first of Ivan Grozny's seven consecutive wives was Anastasia Romanov (d. 1560).

The Romanov line was the second (and last) dynasty in Russian history, lasting until the abdication of Nicholas II in 1917. Mikhail's reign (1613–45) was marked by the completion of the Russian drive across Siberia, when Cossacks reached Okhotsk on the Pacific. Mikhail's son Alexis followed him to the throne in 1645. Alexis was responsible for solidifying rigid ties of dependence between lords and peasants, contributing to the process of en-serfment of free Russian agricultural workers that had been occurring for centuries. Alexis' jurists produced the Ulozhenie in 1649, which established that serfs were a hereditary class. Thus, while serfdom was disappearing in Western Europe it was expanding in Russia, setting the stage for radical political movements in the coming centuries, the goal of which activity was frequently the alleviation of the serfs' suffering. Alexis faced two social up-heavals during his reign, the first of which was caused by the ecclesiastical reforms of Patriarch Nikon. In 1654, a schism emerged in the Russian church over Nikon's reforms, with one large group of dissenters led by Ar-chpriest Avvakum insisting on the legitimacy of the old rituals which Nikon wished to eliminate in order to bring the Russian church into line with that of Constantinople. Thus were born the "Old Believers" or "Old Ritualists," who still practice their peculiar variety of Russian Orthodoxy.

The second major problem which Alexis faced was the revolt of the Cos-sack Stenka Razin, which took on overtones of a class conflict when peas-ants joined the uprising. Alexis, however, was capable of successfully weathering his political storms, and the Romanovs proved to be one of the most powerful ruling families in all of Europe in the eighteenth century.

The first passage in this section is "The Lament of Boris Godunov's Daughter," a bylina recorded by the Anglican chaplain to the English com-mercial expedition to Russia in 1619, Richard James, translated by W. R. Morfill. The second passage is another bylina recorded by Richard James, "The Return of Patriarch Filaret to Moscow," which describes the return of Mikhail Romanov's father from his Lithuanian captivity (1619), when he was elevated to the patriarchate. The text is translated by Leo Wiener. The fourth passage consists of excerpts from the Ulozhenie, edited by George Vernad-sky and Ralph T. Fisher.

Our final passage consists of brief excerpts from the autobiography of Archpriest Avvakum, describing his early life and his calling to the priest-hood, which experience would have been similar for many of the priests of the Russian Orthodox Church.

.

✤ *The Lament of Boris Godunov's Daughter*[1]

"The little bird laments,
The white quail,
Oh! how must I weep, young as I am—
They are going to burn the vigorous oak,
To destroy my little nest,
To kill my little fledglings,
And to capture me, the quail.
The Tsarevna weeps in Moscow,
Alas! I, the youthful, must mourn
Because the traitor is coming to Moscow,
Grishka Otrepiev, the unfrocked priest,
Who wishes to take me prisoner,
And having imprisoned me, to make me a nun,
And to put me among those who wear black robes;
But I do not wish to be a nun,
Or to wear the black robe—
The dark cell must be thrown open,
So that I may see the youths in their bravery,
Alas! for our pleasant greetings:
Who will come among you
After us, with our lordly lives,
And after the Tsar Boris.
Thus the Tsarevna weeps in Moscow,
The daughter of Boris Godunov—
O God, merciful Saviour,
Why is our empire destroyed?
It is for the sins of my father,
For my mother's lack of prayer."

---

1. Reprinted from W. R. Morfill, *The Story of Russia* (New York, G. P. Putnam's Sons, 1890), p. 101.

Photo: Icon of St. Dmitri the Tsarevich and Prince Roman of Uglich. Moscow Court School, first third of the Seventeenth Century.

✥ *The Return of Filaret to Moscow*[1]

The Tsardom of Muscovy was happy
and all the holy Russian land.
Happy was the sovereign, the Orthodox tsar,
the Grand Duke Mikhail Fedorovich,
for he was told that his father had arrived,
his father Filaret Nikitich,
from the land of the infidel, from Lithuania.
He had brought back with him many princes and boyars,
he had also brought the boyar of the tsar,
Prince Mikhail Borisovich Sheyn.
There had come together many princes, boyars, and dignitaries,
in the mighty Tsardom of Muscovy;
They wished to meet Filaret Nikitich
outside the famous white stone-built Moscow.
'Tis not the beautiful sun in its orbit—
'tis the Orthodox tsar that has gone out,
to meet his father dear,
Lord Filaret Nikitich.
With the tsar went his uncle,
Ivan Nikitich the boyar—
    "The Lord grant my father be well,
    my father, Lord Filaret Nikitich."
They went not into the palace of the tsar,
they went into the cathedral of the most Holy Virgin,
to sing a holy Mass.
And he blessed his beloved child:
    "God grant the Orthodox tsar be well,
    Grand Duke Mikhail Fedorovich!
    And for him to rule the Tsardom of Muscovy
    and the holy Russian land."

---

1. Reprinted from Leo Weiner, *Anthology of Russian Literature* (New York, Benjamin Blom, 1967), pt. 1, pp. 133–134.

✣ The Ulozhenie of 1649[1]

[From the Introduction:]

In the year 156 [1648], on the sixteenth day of July, the sovereign tsar and grand prince Aleksei Mikkhailovich . . . took counsel with his [spiritual] father who prays for him, the most holy Joseph, patriarch of Moscow and all Russia . . . and with the entire holy council, and decided together with his boyars and okol'nichie and [other] Duma members [dumnye liudi]: that any articles written in the rules of the holy apostles and the holy fathers and in the civil laws of the Greek tsars [Byzantine emperors] pertaining to affairs of state and of the land should be copied out: and that the decrees of the former great sovereigns, tsars, and grand princes of Russia and the boyar resolutions . . . regarding various affairs of state and of the land should be compiled; and that these sovereign decrees and boyar resolutions should be compared with the old codes of law [sudebniki, referring to the sudebniki of 1497 and 1550, and perhaps also the draft code of 1589.] And as for matters that were not previously covered in the codes of law, by the decrees of former sovereigns, and on which there have been no boyar resolutions, articles [on these matters] should likewise be written down and presented for common discussion, in accordance with his sovereign decree, so that the dispensation of justice in the Muscovite state shall in all cases be equal for men of every rank, from the highest rank to the lowest. And the sovereign ordered . . . the boyars Prince Nikita Ivanovich Odoevskii and Prince Semen Vasil'evich Prozorovskii, and the okol'nichii Prince Fedor Fedorovich Volkonskii, and the secretaries Gavrila Levont'ev and Fedor Griboedov, to compile everything and to submit it in written form.

And for this great sovereign act of state and of the land, the sovereign ordered, upon taking counsel with the patriarch of Moscow and all Russia, and the boyars resolved, that from among the stol'niki and striapchie and Moscow dvoriane and zhil'tsy, two men shall be chosen from each rank; likewise that from among the dvoriane and deti boiarskie of all the provinces [gorod; but here used to mean the entire territory of which the town was the administrative center], two men shall be taken from each greater province, except Novgorod; and from Novgorod, one man from each fifth [*piatina*, one of the five territorial divisions]; and from the lesser provinces, one man

---

1. Reprinted by permission of the publishers from George Vernadsky, Ralph T. Fisher, Alan D. Ferguson, Andrew Losky, and Sergei Pushkarev, *A Source Book for Russian History from Early Times to 1917* (New Haven, Yale University Press, 1972), v. 1, pp. 223–228. We have preserved within the text the bracketed helpful information provided by the translators.

each; and from among the gosti, three men; and from the gostinaia and suk-onnaia sotni [in Moscow], two men each; and from the chernye sotni and slobody [in Moscow], and from the posad in each town, one man each: good and sensible men, so as to confirm and arrange, with all these elected deputies, this sovereign act of state and of the land, so that henceforth all these great acts, in accordance with his present sovereign decree and the statutes of the sobor, shall remain inviolate.

In accordance with the sovereign's . . . decree, the boyars Prince Nikita Ivanovich Odoevskii and his associates, having copied out [articles] from the rules of the holy apostles and the holy fathers, from the civil laws of the Greek tsars, and from the old codes of law of former great sovereigns, and from the decrees . . . of the tsar and grand prince of all Russia Mikhail Feodorovich, and from the boyar resolutions, and articles [on matters] that were not included in the former codes of law and in decrees of former sovereigns and in boyar resolutions, wrote down [all] these articles anew and brought them before the sovereign.

And in the current year, 157 [still 1648, since the year 7157 began on September 1], on the third day of October, the tsar . . . with his father who prays for him, the most holy Joseph, patriarch of Moscow and all Russia, and with the metropolitans, and with the archbishops and with the bishops, and likewise with the sovereign's boyars, and with the okol'nichie, and with the [other] Duma members, listened to this compilation; and it was read to the elected deputies who had been chosen in Moscow and from the towns to this general sobor, so that this entire ulozhenie should henceforth be permanent and immutable. And the sovereign ordered that a transcript of this entire ulozhenie be drawn upon and that this transcript be ratified by the most holy Joseph, patriarch of Moscow . . . and by the entire holy council, and by the sovereign's boyars and okol'nichie and [other] Duma members, and by the elected deputies from the dvoriane, deti boiarskie, gosti, and trading and posad men of the Muscovite state and of all the towns of the Russian tsardom. After the ulozhenie had been ratified by the signatures [of those persons], the sovereign ordered that it be copied into a book, and that this book be certified by the signatures of the secretaries Gavrila Levont'ev and Fedor Griboedov; and that many copies of this book be printed for use in all the prikazy in Moscow, and in the towns, and that all affairs be conducted in accordance with this ulozhenie.

And in accordance with the decree of the sovereign tsar and grand prince of all Russia Aleksei Mikhailovich, a transcript of this ulozhenie was drawn up. The most holy Joseph, patriarch of Moscow and all Russia . . . and the entire holy council, and likewise the boyars and okol'nichie and [other]

Duma members, and the elected dvoriane, deti boiarskie, gosti, and trading [and] posad men, affixed their signatures to the transcript of this ulozhenie. . . .

[Sections from the Ulozhenie proper:]

CHAPTER VII

8. Whoever of the sovereign's soldiers of any rank are in the sovereign's service in the regiments, and who, having been examined, are [found] capable of serving the sovereign but who desert the sovereign's service without waiting for discharge, to them shall be applied the rule for desertion; whoever deserts a first time shall be beaten with the knout; if he deserts a second time, he shall again be beaten with the knout, and his emolument in pomest'e land shall be reduced . . . and if he deserts a third time, he shall again be beaten with the knout, and his pomest'e shall be taken away and given for distribution [to others]. . . .

17. If any service men petition the sovereign that they are incapable of serving the sovereign because of age, or injuries, or sickness . . . these petitioners shall be examined in Moscow and in the towns. And if the examination shows that these service men are truly incapable of serving the sovereign because of age, or injuries, or sickness, those service men shall be ordered to send in their place to serve the sovereign, with all their retinue and equipment, those of their children, brothers, nephews, and grandsons who have no pomest'ia and who, being eighteen years of age, are old enough to serve the sovereign but are not in the sovereign's service and are not enrolled in any rank; but they shall send no one to serve in their place who is under eighteen years of age. And if they have no such children or brothers or nephews or grandsons, and if they themselves are incapable of serving the sovereign in any way, because of sickness or age: from them recruits or money shall be taken for the sovereign's service, in proportion to [the size of] their pomest'ia and patrimonies and to their means. . . .

CHAPTER VIII

1. For ransoming captives [most of whom were seized by the Tatars in their perennial raids], money shall be collected yearly from the towns of the entire Muscovite state: from the posad households and from the post riders, and from all the inhabitants who live in the towns in posady . . . and from the peasants and *bobyli* [peasants without plowland, or with small holdings, and thus not bearing tiaglo] on monastery estates—eight den'gi [den'ga—a small silver coin worth half a copeck] from each household; and from peasants living in the sovereign's crown villages, and in the chernye volosti [inhabited by tiaglo-bearing peasants], and on pomest'ia and patrimonial

estates—four den'gi from each household; and from the service men, from the strel'tsy, cannoneers, stockade tenders, and gate guards and from the state carpenters and blacksmiths, and from sundry service men—two den'gi from each household. This money shall be paid yearly into the Ambassadorial Prikaz . . . so that no one should be exempt from this monetary levy, since such ransoming is called an act of common charity. . . .

CHAPTER X

1. The judicial authority of the sovereign tsar and grand prince of all Russia Aleksei Mikhailovich shall be exercised by the boyars and okol'nichie and [other] Duma members and secretaries, and by the various government officials and judges; and justice shall be dispensed equitably to all men of the Muscovite state, from the highest rank to the lowest. . . .

2. Lawsuits that for any reason cannot be decided in the prikazy shall be taken out of the prikazy and submitted to the sovereign tsar and grand prince of all Russia Aleksei Mikhailovich, and to his, the sovereign's, boyars and okol'nichie and [other] Duma members. And the boyars and okol'nichie and [other] Duma members shall sit in the chamber and, in accordance with the sovereign's decree, shall decide such cases jointly. . . .

CHAPTER XI

1. Peasants and bobyli of the sovereign's crown villages and chernye volosti who have fled from the sovereign's crown villages and from the chernye volosti, and who live with the patriarch [i.e. on his land] . . . or with the monasteries, or with boyars . . . or with various owners of patrimonies and pomest'ia, and who themselves, or whose fathers, are registered on the sovereign's in the registry books with the registrars have submitted to the Pomestnyi Prikaz and other prikazy since the Moscow fire of the year 7134 [1626]: these, the sovereign's fugitive peasants and bobyli, shall be found and returned, with their wives and children and with all their peasant possessions, to the sovereign's crown villages and to the chernye volosti, to their old plots in accordance with the registry books, without time limit.

2. Likewise, if any owner of a patrimony or pomest'e petitions the sovereign concerning his fugitive peasants and bobyli . . . these peasants and bobyli shall be returned upon investigation, in accordance with the registry books. . . . And fugitive peasants and bobyli shall be returned from flight to men [their owners] of every rank, in accordance with the registry books, without time limit.

3. And whomever it falls upon to return fugitive peasants and bobyli, upon court decision and investigation, shall return these peasants with their wives and children and with all their possessions, and with their harvested and unharvested grain. . . .

9. And whatever peasants and bobyli are listed with anyone [a landowner] in the census books of the previous years of 154 and 155 [1646 and 1647], and who subsequent to [the compilation of] these census books have fled, or shall henceforth flee, from those men with whom they are listed in the census books: those fugitive peasants and bobyli, and their brothers, children, nephews, and grandchildren with their wives and with their children and with all their possessions, and with their harvested and unharvested grain, shall be returned from flight to those men from whom they fled, in accordance with the census books, without time limit; and henceforth under no circumstances should anyone receive peasants who are not his and keep them with him.

10. And if anyone, subsequent to [the promulgation of] this sovereign ulozhenie, should receive fugitive peasants and bobyli, and their children and brothers and nephews, and keep them with him, and if the pomest'e and patrimony owners discover these, their fugitive peasants, with him, . . . that person shall pay ten rubles for each peasant for every year, as restitution for the sovereign's taxes and the pomest'e-owner's income; and he shall give [this money] to the plaintiff who owns these peasants and bobyli. . . .

30. And the pomest'e and patrimony owners with whom peasants and bobyli . . . are registered on their pomest'e and patrimonial land separately shall not remove their peasants from their pomest'e land to their patrimonal land and thereby depopulate their pomest'ia. . . .

CHAPTER XIII

1. Prior to [the promulgation of] the present sovereign ulozhenie, lawsuits involving metropolitans . . . and abbots . . . and church servitors were in every case conducted in the prikaz of the Great Palace [Bol'shogo Dvortsa, primarily in charge of the tsar's household].

But now the sovereign, tsar, and grand prince of all Russia Aleksei Mikhailovich, upon the petition of the stol'niki, and striapchie, and Moscow dvoriane, and provincial dvoriane and deti boiarskie, and gosti, and the gostinaia and sukonnaia and various other sotni and slobody, and the trading and posad men of the towns, has decreed that there be a separate Monastery Prikaz, and that all lawsuits brought by plaintiffs against metropolitans . . . and monasteries . . . and priests, and church servitors shall be tried in the Monastery Prikaz. . . .

[Article 61 of chapter XVI established that aged and disabled dvoriane and deti boiarskie who were childless could hold their pomest'ia in lifetime tenure and send recruits to serve in their place.]

CHAPTER XVII

42. . . . The sovereign tsar . . . has ordered and the sobor has decreed that after the promulgation of the present ulozhenie the patriarch, metropolitans, archbishops, bishops, and monasteries shall not buy ancestral, or service-earned, or purchased patrimonies from anyone, or take them in mortgage, or hold them in possession, or under any circumstances take them for the eternal commemoration of souls; . . . and no patrimony owner shall give his patrimony to a monastery. . . .

CHAPTER XIX

1. Whatever slobody in Moscow belong to the patriarch and the metropolitans and bishops and monasteries, and boyars and okol'nichie and [other] Duma members and closest advisers, and men of every rank, and are inhabited by tradesmen and artisans who are engaged in various trades and keep shops but do not pay taxes to the sovereign and are not in [his] service, all these slobody, with all the men who live in these slobody, except for contractual bondmen, shall all be made to bear tiaglo to the sovereign and to serve him eternally and immutably. . . .

5. And whatever slobody near Moscow belong to the patriarch and prelates and monasteries, and boyars and [other] Duma members and men of every rank, these slobody with all their men who are engaged in various trades, except for contractual bondmen, shall likewise be taken for the sovereign upon investigation. As for plowland peasants, if any of them are found upon questioning to be old-time peasants of pomest'ia and patrimonies, who have been brought to these lands [the slobody], those men from whom these slobody are taken shall be ordered to remove [the peasants] from these slobody to their patrimonies and pomest'ia. And if these plowland peasants keep shops, cellars, and salterns in Moscow and in the towns, they shall sell these shops, cellars, and salterns to men who bear the sovereign's tiaglo, and henceforth no one who does not bear the sovereign's tiaglo shall keep shops, cellars, and salterns. . . .

11. And whatever strel'tsy, Cossacks, and dragoons engage in various trading enterprises and keep shops in the towns, these strel'tsy, Cossacks, and dragoons shall pay customs duties on their trading enterprises, and obrok on their shops, but shall not pay tiaglo with the posad men or be subject to tiaglo service.

13. As for those tiaglo-bearing posad men in Moscow and in the towns who themselves, or whose fathers, formerly lived in the posady and slobody

of Moscow or in the towns, and were obliged to pay and did not pay tiaglo, or who lived in posady and slobody as shop clerks or hired hands of tiaglo-bearing men, but who at present live in pledge to the patriarch, the metropolitans, the archbishops, the bishops, the monasteries, the boyars . . . and to men of every rank in Moscow and in the towns, on their homesteads and on patrimonies, and on pomest'ia and on church land; they shall all be sought out and returned, permanently and irrevocably, to their old posad places, wherever each one formerly lived. And henceforth no men who are taken for the sovereign shall enroll themselves in pledge to anyone or call themselves anyone's peasants or bondmen [liudi]. If henceforth they should pledge themselves· to anyone, or call themselves anyone's peasants or bondmen, for this they shall be severely punished, beaten with the knout in the market-place, and banished to Siberia to live on the Lena River. And those men who henceforth receive them in pledge shall likewise be in the sovereign's great disfavor, and the lands where such men should henceforth come to live in pledge to them shall be taken for the sovereign. . . .

15. And whatever bondmen and peasants of boyars and men of other ranks, in Moscow and in the towns, have bought or taken in mortgage tiaglo-bearing homesteads, shops, storehouses, stone cellars, and salterns, and who trade in various goods, these bondmen and peasants of boyars and men of other ranks shall sell these tiaglo-bearing homesteads, shops, cellars, storehouses, and salterns to tiaglo-bearing trading and posad men; and henceforth they shall not own tiaglo-bearing homesteads, shops, cellars, storehouses, or salterns; and henceforth no one's bondmen or peasants, but only the sovereign's trading posad men, shall buy tiaglo-bearing homesteads, shops, cellars, storehouses, or salterns from anyone. . . .

17. And whatever peasants come to Moscow and to the towns from the country with various goods, they shall sell these goods in the market square from carts and barges, freely and without payment [of impost]; but they shall not buy or rent shops in the market rows. . . .

39. . . . Tiaglo-bearing men belonging to chernye sotni and to slobody of tiaglo-bearing homesteads shall not mortgage or sell their homesteads to men who do not bear tiaglo. If anyone sells or mortgages a tiaglo-bearing homestead to "white" men [who do not bear tiaglo], these homesteads shall be taken and returned to the sotnia without recompense. . . . And if any tiaglo-bearing men sell or mortgage their homesteads, these tiaglo-bearing men shall be beaten with the knout for their offense.

40. And whatever homesteads belong to Russian men of every rank in Moscow, in Kitai- or Belyi- or Zemlianoi-gorod [and] in suburban slobody, these homesteads and homestead plots shall not be bought or taken in mortgage from Russian men by foreigners or foreign widows. . . . And as for the foreign churches that have been erected on foreign homesteads, these churches shall be torn down, and henceforth no churches shall stand on for-

eign homesteads in Kitai- or Belyi- or Zemlianoi-gorod, but they shall stand beyond the city, beyond Zemlianoi-gorod, far away from the [Orthodox] churches of God.

CHAPTER XX

2. Henceforth no one shall take deti boiarskie as bondmen whether they have been classified for service or not.

31. And whoever is registered in bondage by a title-deed, these people shall transmit their bondage from wife to husband, and from husband to wife. . . .

34. And if anyone's bondman is taken captive into some other land, and afterward this bondman leaves captivity, he shall no longer be the bondman of his former master, and his wife and children shall be returned to him for his sufferings as a captive. . . .

52. And whatever men keep bondmen in accordance with their father's contracts, after their fathers have died, they shall their father's men free; and these men shall be the bondmen of him to whom they give, of their free will, a contract of servitude upon themselves.

70. And unbaptized [non-Orthodox] foreigners in Moscow and in the towns may keep foreigners of various and sundry faiths to work in their households; but Russian men shall not be in bondage to unbaptized foreigners, whether by title-deeds or of their own will. . . .

113. . . . In accordance with the sovereign's decree, it is forbidden for anyone to take contracts [of servitude] from his peasants or his peasants' children.

CHAPTER XXI

3. The criminal judges [tseloval'niki] shall have jurisdiction in the towns over cases of robbery, murder, and theft, in accordance with instructions from the Criminal [Razboinyi] Prikaz, and the voevody shall have no jurisdiction over such matters in towns. But where there are no criminal judges, in those towns the voevody and government officials shall have jurisdiction over criminal cases.

4. The criminal judges for such matters in the towns should be good and prosperous dvoriane, who have been discharged from service because of age or wounds, or whose children or nephews serve in their place, and who can read and write; but those who cannot read and write should not be chosen as criminal judges. As for towns where there are no dvoriane, in those towns deti boiarskie who are likewise good and prosperous men shall be chosen as criminal judges. . . . And the criminal judges in the towns shall be chosen

by the dvoriane, deti boiarskie, posad men, town inhabitants [zhiletskie liudi] of every rank, and district cadastral peasants, and the dvoriane, deti boiarskie, posad men, town inhabitants of every rank, and district peasants shall certify the election of these criminal judges with their signatures . . . and the criminal judges in the towns shall have sworn assistants and clerks with them for cases of robbery and theft, and the prisons shall have prison guards; they shall likewise be chosen by the cadastral peasants and shall take an oath upon the cross.

✥ *Avvakum's Calling*[1]

I was born in the region of Nizhny-Novgorod, beyond the river Kudna, in the village of Grigorovo. My father, Peter by name, was a priest. My mother, Maria, took the veil under the name of Martha. My father was given to drink, but my mother practised prayer and fasting and constantly taught me the fear of God.

One day I saw a neighbor's ox fall dead, and that night I arose and wept before the holy icon, sorrowing for my soul and meditating upon death, since I likewise should die. From that time on it became my custom to pray each night. . .

My mother decided that I should marry. I besought the Mother of God to give me a wife who would help me attain salvation . . . there was a maiden, also an orphan, who was wont to go frequently to church, and whose name was Anastasia. Her father was the blacksmith, Marco, a rich man; but after his death his whole substance was wasted.

The maiden lived in poverty, and she prayed to God that she might be united to me in marriage; and it was God's will that this should come about. Then my mother returned to God after a life of great piety, and as for me, being turned out, I went to live in another place. I was ordained deacon at the age of twenty and priest two years later.

Bibliography

From the vast number of works concerning Moscow through the early Romanovs, see the following:

---

1. Avvakum's autobiography has been widely reproduced. These excerpts are from G. P. Fedotov, ed. and Helen Iswolsky, trans., *A Treasury of Russian Spirituality* (New York, Sheed and Ward, Inc., 1948), pp. 137–38.

Benson, Bobrick, *Fearful Majesty: The Life and Reign of Ivan the Terrible* (New York, 1987).

Horace W. Dewey, "Tales of Moscow's Founding," in *Canadian-American Slavic Studies* 6 (1972).

Stephen Graham, *Boris Godunof* (New Haven, 1933).

Ian Grey, *Ivan III and the Unification of Russia* (London, 1964).

Philip Longworth, *Alexis, Tsar of All the Russias* (New York, 1984).

Ihor Ševčenko, "A Neglected Byzantine Source of Muscovite Political Ideology," in *Harvard Slavic Studies* 2 (1954).

Questions to Consider

1. In what ways was the political ideology of Moscow different from that of all previous Russian polities?

2. What were the views of Russian monastic authors concerning the union of the Roman Catholic and Greek Orthodox churches that was engineered at the Council of Ferrera/Florence (1439)?

3. According to Kurbsky, how did Ivan *Grozny's* character or personality influence his style of political leadership?

4. Why might the English translation of Ivan's epithet *Grozny* as "the Dread" or as "the Terrible" be appropriate?

5. What was the significance of the commercial contacts between English and Russian merchants during Ivan Grozny's reign, from the perspective of politics as well as economics?

6. Why were the years between the reign of Boris Gudunov and Mikhail Romanov called the "Time of Troubles?"

7. What does the *Ulozhenie* reveal of the nature of Muscovite society during the reign of Alexis and the early Romanovs?

8. By comparing it with Yaroslav's *Pravda* and the *Charter of Novgorod,* show how the *Ulozhenie* reflects an attempt to create a centralized monarchy in Russia.

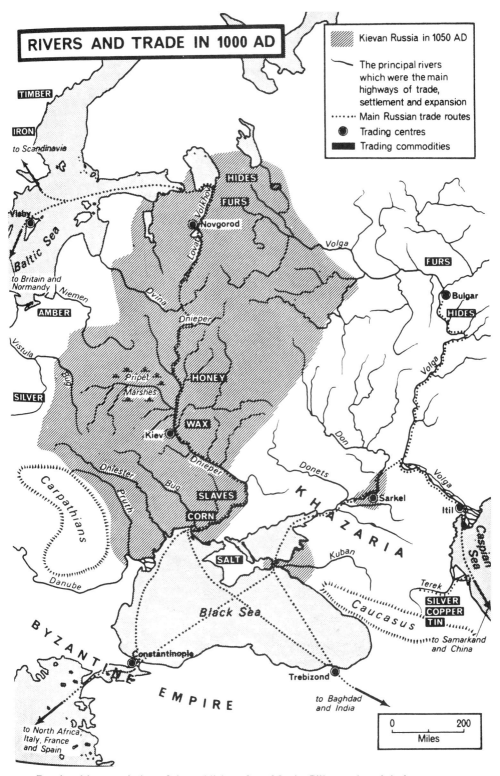

RIVERS AND TRADE IN 1000 AD

/////	Kievan Russia in 1050 AD
——	The principal rivers which were the main highways of trade, settlement and expansion
......	Main Russian trade routes
●	Trading centres
■	Trading commodities

TIMBER

IRON

to Scandinavia

HIDES

FURS

Visby

Novgorod

Volkhov

Lovat

Volga

FURS

Baltic Sea

to Britain and Normandy

Niemen

Dvina

Bulgar

HIDES

AMBER

Dnieper

Bug

Vistula

SILVER

Pripet Marshes

HONEY

Volga

WAX

Kiev

Dnieper

Don

Donets

Carpathians

Dniester

Prut

Bug

SLAVES

CORN

K H A Z A R I A

Sarkel

Volga

Itil

SALT

Kuban

Caspian Sea

Danube

Black Sea

Caucasus

Terek

SILVER
COPPER
TIN

to Samarkand and China

B Y Z A N T I N E   E M P I R E

Constantinople

Trebizond

to Baghdad and India

to North Africa, Italy, France and Spain

0	200

Miles

Reprinted by permission of the publishers from Martin Gilbert, ed. and Arthur Banks, cartographer, *Atlas of Russian History* (New York, The Dorset Press, 1985), p. 14.

THE FRAGMENTATION OF KIEVAN RUSSIA 1054–1238

0   200
Miles

DEPENDENCIES OF NOVGOROD

FINNS

Ustiug

Ladoga

Belozersk

VLADIMIR–SUZDAL

Reval

REPUBLIC
OF NOVGOROD
● Novgorod

Kostroma●

● Yaroslavl
● Rostov

VOLGA
BULGARS

● Pskov

Torzhok ●

●Suzdal

Riga

Izborsk

Tver
●

Moscow

Vladimir

Muron

Baltic Sea

LITHUANIA

Dvina

Polotsk ●

SMOLENSK
Viazma●

Riazan

**MUROM-
RIAZAN**

Kovno ●

Vitebsk ●

Smolensk

POLOTSK
● Minsk

CHERNIGOV

Vistula

● Bialystok

TUROV
● Pinsk

Turov

Chernigov ●

**NOVGOROD-
SEVERSK**

POLAND

VOLHYNIA

KIEV
Kiev ●

● Pereyaslavl

PEREYASLAVL

Cracow

● Zhitomir

GALICIA
● Galich

Dniester

Don

Carpathians

CUMANS or POLOVTSI

HUNGARY

*Black
Sea*

On the death of Yaroslav in 1054, Kievan Russia
was divided among his sons. Their constant
feuds led to the fragmentation of the once
powerful kingdom. United briefly from 1113 to 1125
by Vladimir Monomakh, the Russian lands were again
divided and in conflict during the hundred years
before the Mongol invasion of 1238. In 1199 Galicia
and Volhynia were united, and in 1254 recognised
by the Pope as an independent kingdom. In
1307 Polotsk came under Lithuanian suzerainty

Constantinople ●

▭ The twelve Principalities
of Russia in 1100

Reprinted by permission of the publishers from **Martin Gilbert**, ed. and **Arthur
Banks**, cartographer, *Atlas of Russian History* (New York, The Dorset Press, 1985),
p. 17.

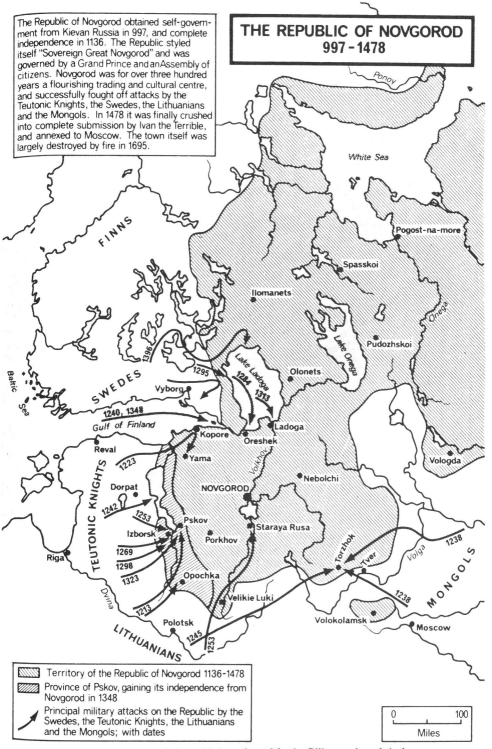

The Republic of Novgorod obtained self-government from Kievan Russia in 997, and complete independence in 1136. The Republic styled itself "Sovereign Great Novgorod" and was governed by a Grand Prince and an Assembly of citizens. Novgorod was for over three hundred years a flourishing trading and cultural centre, and successfully fought off attacks by the Teutonic Knights, the Swedes, the Lithuanians and the Mongols. In 1478 it was finally crushed into complete submission by Ivan the Terrible, and annexed to Moscow. The town itself was largely destroyed by fire in 1695.

THE REPUBLIC OF NOVGOROD
997 - 1478

White Sea

Ponoy

FINNS

SWEDES

Baltic Sea

Gulf of Finland

Reval

TEUTONIC KNIGHTS

Dorpat

Riga

Dvina

LITHUANIANS

Pogost-na-more

Spasskoi

Ilomanets

Lake Ladoga

Lake Onega

Onega

Pudozhskoi

Olonets

1396

1295

1284

1313

Vyborg

1240, 1348

Kopore

Oreshek

Ladoga

Volkhov

Vologda

Yama

1223

Nebolchi

NOVGOROD

1242

1253

Pskov

Izborsk

Porkhov

Staraya Rusa

1269

1298

1323

Opochka

Torzhok

Tver

Volga

1238

MONGOLS

1213

Velikie Luki

1238

Polotsk

1245

1253

Volokolamsk

Moscow

▨ Territory of the Republic of Novgorod 1136-1478

▨ Province of Pskov, gaining its independence from Novgorod in 1348

⬈ Principal military attacks on the Republic by the Swedes, the Teutonic Knights, the Lithuanians and the Mongols; with dates

0   100
Miles

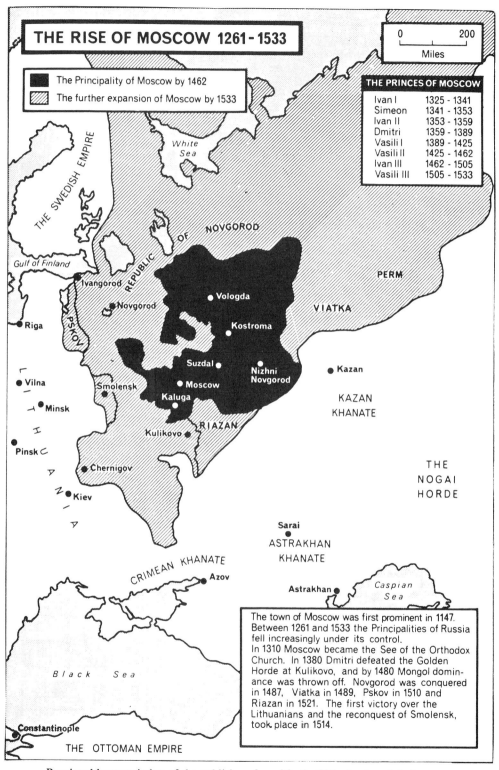

THE RISE OF MOSCOW 1261-1533

0	200
	Miles

■ The Principality of Moscow by 1462

▨ The further expansion of Moscow by 1533

THE PRINCES OF MOSCOW

Ivan I	1325 - 1341
Simeon	1341 - 1353
Ivan II	1353 - 1359
Dmitri	1359 - 1389
Vasili I	1389 - 1425
Vasili II	1425 - 1462
Ivan III	1462 - 1505
Vasili III	1505 - 1533

THE SWEDISH EMPIRE

White Sea

Gulf of Finland

REPUBLIC OF NOVGOROD

Ivangorod

Novgorod

PERM

Riga

PSKOV

VIATKA

Vologda

Kostroma

Vilna

Suzdal

Nizhni Novgorod

Kazan

Smolensk

Moscow

KAZAN KHANATE

Minsk

Kaluga

RIAZAN

Pinsk

Kulikovo

THE NOGAI HORDE

Chernigov

Kiev

Sarai

ASTRAKHAN KHANATE

CRIMEAN KHANATE

Azov

Astrakhan

Caspian Sea

Black Sea

The town of Moscow was first prominent in 1147. Between 1261 and 1533 the Principalities of Russia fell increasingly under its control.
In 1310 Moscow became the See of the Orthodox Church. In 1380 Dmitri defeated the Golden Horde at Kulikovo, and by 1480 Mongol dominance was thrown off. Novgorod was conquered in 1487, Viatka in 1489, Pskov in 1510 and Riazan in 1521. The first victory over the Lithuanians and the reconquest of Smolensk, took place in 1514.

Constantinople

THE OTTOMAN EMPIRE

Reprinted by permission of the publishers from Martin Gilbert, ed. and Arthur Banks, cartographer, *Atlas of Russian History* (New York, The Dorset Press, 1985), p. 25.

Glossary

Bloodwite. A fine for murder payable to the prince.

Boyar. A member of the landed medieval Russian aristocracy (i.e., whose wealth was derived from the land he held).

Chiliarch. A commander of a thousand men.

Denga. A medieval Russian monetary unit (borrowed from Mongolian), of which one was the equivalent of one-half of a *copek.* In modern Russian the term means "money."

Deti Boyarskie. Collective term for the petty nobility, whose status was usually derived from service, rather than land.

Dvorianin. A courtier or a nobleman.

Grivna. A medieval Russian monetary unit which was the equivalent of twenty *dengas.*

Igumen. An abbot of an Orthodox monastery.

Izgoi. A serf dependent on a landed aristocrat.

Kholop. A slave.

Kniaz. A prince.

Liudin. A commoner.

Mir. A community or township.

Muzh. A nobleman or warrior aristocrat.

Nogata. A monetary unit, which was the equivalent of one-twentieth of a *grivna.*

Oprichnina. Area of Russia in which paramilitary service aristocracy dominated during the reign of Ivan IV.

Pomestie. An estate granted to a warrior aristocrat in return for military service.

Prikaz. A department of the government in Moscow.

Rezana. A monetary unit, which was the equivalent of one-fiftieth of a *grivna.*

Ruble. A monetary unit, which was the equivalent of two hundred *dengas.*

Sloboda.   Section of town whose inhabitants were taxpayers.

Sobor.   An assembly.

Stolnik.   Courtier who attended the Tsar' specifically when foreign visitors were present.

Sukonnaia Sotnia.   Association of textile merchants in Moscow.

Tiaglo.   Tax paid by urban and rural inhabitants.

Veche.   A village or city assembly.

Vladyka. A master (secular) or prelate (religious).

Voevoda.   A military and administrative leader.

Votchina.   A hereditary form of landowning.

Zemskii Sobor.   An assembly of the landed aristocracy.